TEGOTOMONO

Music for the Japanese Koto

BONNIE C. WADE

TEGOTOMONO

Music for the Japanese Koto

Contributions in Intercultural and Comparative Studies, Number 2

GREENWOOD PRESS
Westport, Connecticut
London, England

FOR THE MAKERS OF *KOTOS* AND *KOTO* MUSIC

Library of Congress Cataloging in Publication Data

Wade, Bonnie C
    Tegotomono.

    (Contributions in intercultural and comparative studies ; no. 2)
    Bibliography: p.
    Discography: p.
    Includes index.
    1. Koto music—History and criticism. 2. Music, Japanese—History and criticism.
I. Title
ML234.W23   787'.9   76-5265
ISBN 0-8371-8908-X

Grateful acknowledgment is made to Grove Press, Inc., for permission to reprint
the translation of the poem "Awajishima" from *Anthology of Japanese Literature*,
by Donald Keene © 1955, Grove Press, Inc.; to Stanford University Press for permission to reprint the translation of the poem "Yo no naka ni" from *Japanese
Court Poetry*, by Robert H. Brower and Earl Miner © 1961, Stanford University
Press; to Charles E. Tuttle, Co., for permission to reprint the translation of the
machinuta "Takasago ya" from *The Noh Drama*, Nippon Gakujutsu Shinkokai
© 1955, Charles E. Tuttle, Co.

Library of Congress Catalog Card Number: 76-5265
ISBN: 0-8371-8908-X

Greenwood Press, Inc.
51 Riverside Avenue, Westport, Connecticut 06880

Printed in the United States of America

/ Contents

List of Charts

/ Acknowledgments

The preparation of a work such as this is never a singular achievement. In the course of preparing and writing this book I incurred numerous debts which I can no more than acknowledge here with much appreciation: to Ann Briegleb, Archivist of the late Institute of Ethnomusicology and presently archivist in the UCLA Department of Music, and her staff, who acquired primary materials from Japan and otherwise gave enthusiastic aid to my project; Mrs. Nakako Memon, of Tokyo and Harvard Universities, for her help with scholarly textual translations; Shawn O'Malley, of the UCLA Department of Oriental Languages, for his excellent poetic translations; Professors Pauline Alderman, David Morton, Boris Kremenliev, Robert Tusler, and Ensho Ashikaga for their guidance and invaluable instruction; and my Pescatello family, especially Ann, whose help has been invaluable in so many ways.

I have some special words of gratitude for some teachers, friends, and colleagues: to the Kishibe-sensei, Shigeo, who has been a valuable friend and source person, and Yori, my first teacher of *koto,* who trained me in the Yamada tradition; to Mitsuru and Ikuko Yuge, who introduced me to the Ikuta tradition at UCLA and made available important source material; and to Yagi-sensei, who furthered my study of the Ikuta tradition. I owe much to the musically attuned students of my Music of Japan classes and my *koto* students, who, year after year, in many intangible ways have helped refine this study.

I owe a most special thanks to William P. Malm. He patiently answered the questions of an eager student and introduced me to the world of Japanese music and the *koto* during my first year in Japan. And he did me the final favor of giving the next-to-last draft of this manuscript a thorough reading. His comments and suggestions on fine points were of much help in the final elaboration of this study.

I want to make two special notes regarding this study. The first is that all of the pieces included in this book are part of a larger repertoire which I have studied on the *koto* since 1963. From 1963 until 1966 my repertoire and course of study were in the tradition of the Yamada-*ryū* which I first studied with Kishibe-Hori in Tōkyo. Since 1966 my study and teaching of the *koto* has been in the Ikuta-*ryū*. The change is not common but was necessitated by the absence of a teacher of Yamada-*ryū* in Los Angeles. It has been extremely valuable for me, in my study of Japanese music, to have worked in both *ryū*.

The second note regards my changing view of the field in which I have chosen to work. When I started as an "official" student of ethnomusicology nearly a decade ago, the study of music within the context of culture then, and in large measure still today, mostly meant the study of the music of a non-Western culture. As such this study reflects my first plateau in ethnomusicology: the analysis of a non-Western music with reference to the cultural contexts in which it was produced. This is a valuable approach in itself, but now it seems to me to be just the first step towards ethnomusicology as I now perceive it: the integrated study of music, society, and culture anywhere.

I want to acknowledge with very special thanks an individual and a "group" to whom, in large measure, this book is dedicated: Mantle Hood, my teacher, colleague, and friend who, through the Institute of Ethnomusicology, first made possible the training of ethno*musicologists* in this country; and the makers of *kotos* and *koto* music for giving the world such a beautiful instrument, such beautiful sounds.

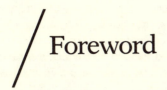

Foreword

This foreword is intended as a foundation, a kind of launch pad for the series sponsored by the Council on Intercultural and Comparative Studies and the Greenwood Press—by commitment already highly significant and in its ultimate potential extremely influential on the direction of the field of intercultural studies.

As the first "ology" ever to use what has become a rather common prefix, namely, "ethno," ethnomusicology has been the pioneer for what would appear to be quite unrelated fields, such as ethnobiology, ethnobotany, ethnohistory, ethnolinguistics, and ethnoscience. But appearances may be deceptive, as we shall show presently. Meanwhile, without laboring shades of difference in application of the prefix in different disciplines, I shall try to set forth what the term "ethnomusicology" has come to mean to the consensus of practicing scholars today.

The term is sometimes incorrectly reserved for the study of musical cultures of the non-Western world, perhaps extended to include the study of folk music, jazz, rock, country Western, and other popular hybrids of the Western world. Subject matter is not necessarily indicative of the meaning that the prefix "ethno" has come to connote in the study of music.

But let me begin nearer the beginning. It is generally accepted, I believe, that the meaning of a term, through time, is likely to change, sometimes radically. The means and methods and even the range of subjects in a discipline can also change, sometimes radically. Both conditions have obtained in the short span of time during which there has been serious scholarly interest in music found all over the world.

In 1968, during the preparation of a manuscript intended as a comprehensive examination of the field, I spoke of a "particular approach to the study of music" rather than a discipline per se, even admitting that it was a field ". . . that has almost as many approaches and objectives as there are [serious] practitioners . . ." (*The Ethnomusicologist,* McGraw-Hill, 1971). The observation was necessary, even though I was and still am totally committed to the approach presented in the book, because at that time there was not yet a clear consensus regarding factors deemed essential to a discipline. Today I believe that has changed.

But let us go back even farther. Charles Seeger has described two epochs in the development of this field, the first dominated by the imposing figure of Eric M. von Hornbostel, the second associated with a formal program of training for which I had responsibility at UCLA.

The first epoch was known as comparative musicology (*vergleichende Musikwissen-*

schaft) and produced a number of distinguished scholars whose primary training was in such diverse fields as linguistics, folklore, acoustics, anthropology, physics, and art history. Most of these scholars studied exotic materials at their desk, rendering transcriptions into European notation from wax cylinders and early disc recordings (usually collected in the field by someone else), making analytical and comparative studies based largely on the standards and aesthetics of European art music. No institutional programs of training for such study were initiated.

The second epoch, known as ethnomusicology, began to emerge in the 1960s as the graduates of the first academic program in ethnomusicology found teaching positions in educational institutions throughout the United States and in many other countries. Earlier, Jaap Kunst had coined the term "ethno-musicology" in an effort to find a more accurate designation for this growing field of concentration. As the training program developed, several factors emerged as being essential to the discipline of ethnomusicology: (1) any music must be studied in its own musical terms and other terms of reference, by its own standards and aesthetics rather than by the arbitrary standards of some other culture, such as the European (an obvious requirement realized in modern linguistics several decades earlier); (2) the study should include the relationship of music to its sociocultural context, including social values and institutions, language, other art forms, history, religion, mores; (3) work in the field, in the laboratory and at the desk, should all be conducted by the same scholar, preferably in collaboration with scholars from other disciplines; (4) field methods *must* include actual participation in the performance of the music under study, that is, learning to play one or more instruments and/or to sing (a basic requirement in the study of any unique mode of discourse, such as speech, music, dance); (5) there must be a constant awareness of the interdependence between and the unique facts within ethnomusicology and many other disciplines—an awareness more likely among musical scholars than among scholars of other disciplines from which the musician can learn and to which he can contribute; (6) fundamental preparation requires a necessarily long and diversified program of academic training.

Now we are ready to speak of application of the term "ethnomusicology." The above approach should be applied to the study of *any* music, found anywhere, at any time through known history, pre- or proto-history, oral history. Such study may center on (1) a particular music, such as Japanese, or even a single aspect of that music, such as koto music of the eighteenth century, or (2) all the musics found in one designated area, such as Los Angeles, Tokyo, Paris, or the Swiss Alps.

This book sets a very high standard, and other authors already under contract and waiting in the wings give promise that this standard will be maintained.

As a final word, I would like to stress the timeliness of this series, its importance and ultimate significance in support of what appears to lie in the immediate future in the field of ethnomusicology. Over the past couple of decades, there has been an accelerating accumulation of significant studies centered on a particular music or an aspect of a particular music. Some of the best of these are to be published in the series. But in my judgment the series is unique in that it also accommodates very nicely what surely lies immediately ahead: interdisciplinary studies designed from an ethnomusicological point of view and directed at large urban areas. There is no concern more pressing than the problem-generating urban center, and there can be no clearer and more significant demonstration of the validity and urgency of collaboration among the arts, humanities, and sciences than in such studies.

Mantle Hood
Honolulu, July 1976

Introduction

It was indeed on the night after the full moon,
in just such a veiled light as Genji had spoken
of, that they visited the Hitachi palace. "I
am afraid," said Myobu, "that it is not a very
good night for listening to music; sounds do
not seem to carry very well." But he would not
be thus put off. "Go to her room," he said,
"and persuade her to play a few notes; it
would be a pity if I went away without hearing
her at all." Myobu . . . found the princess
sitting by the window . . . enjoying the scent
of a blossoming plum-tree. . . . It did indeed
seem just the right moment. "I thought how
lovely your zithern would sound on such a night
as this." . . . [The princess] sent for her
zithern. . . . Timidly she sounded a few notes.
The effect was very agreeable. True, she was
not a great performer; but the instrument was
a particularly fine one and Genji found her
playing by no means unpleasant to listen to.

(From The Tale of Genji, p. 149)

For centuries the plaintive and wistful sounds of
the koto have wafted through misty nights enveloping a
traditional Japanese world. An element of court life
and later a mark of a cultured person and family, the
koto has survived as the premier chamber instrument of
Japanese traditional music. From two planks of beauti-
fully grained pawlonia (kiri) wood the six-foot long
board zither is fashioned by hollowing out one plank to

form the resonating chamber which is then enclosed on
the underside by the second plank. Sounds, at times
soft and harp-like or harsh and percussive, are
produced on the thirteen strings arched tautly and
gracefully across thirteen bridges and along the length
of the instrument.[1] Gentility, refinement, intimate

Koto

moments with music have been its mission, though its
players and its repertoire have changed through time.

Until the twentieth century the repertoire of
music for the koto (sōkyoku) consisted primarily of
three genres: kumiuta, danmono, and tegotomono. This
study is concerned with the last, tegotomono, which was
developed to its present form in the nineteenth century.

Kumiuta, the predominant koto genre in the seventeenth century, was a cycle of six short songs (kumi
"short," uta "song"). The form of each song was strict,
kept to thirty-two measures of 4/4 or 2/4. The role of

[1] For a detailed description of koto construction,
see Adriaansz (1973) Chapter 2. Effort has been made
not to duplicate appreciable amounts of information
given in that excellent source on the koto. Player sits
at far right end of instrument as pictured above, with
back to the reader.

the koto was apparently to follow the vocal line
closely and to interject short interludes (ai-no-te,
the longest twenty-eight to thirty-two beats) between
songs.[2]   Although kumiuta is defined as a cycle of
songs, it has traditionally been classified as an
instrumental genre. Recently, for example, a leading
Japanese musicologist wrote: "The musical form of koto
compositions varies. . . . Most of the pieces are songs.
The oldest style, Kumi-uta, is a song style consisting
of six short songs." (Kishibe 1969: 41) A possible
explanation for such a classification lies in performance practice, for as Kishibe explains: "Kumi-uta was
sung and played by one musician. This manner of performance, that singer and player are to be one and the
same, has been preserved today as the traditional
manner of performing koto music." (1969: 41)

A purely instrumental (shirabemono) genre did
exist in the seventeenth century, however. Danmono
is a type of composition written in sections (dan),
each dan subtly varied from the preceding one. Each
dan is 104 beats long, but the number of sections
varies from danmono to danmono. Unlike kumiuta which
is now seldom heard, danmono are still widely performed
today.[3]

In the eighteenth century the overweaning popularity of lyrical songs -- and therefore of the shamisen
which accompanied them—caused the popularity of the

[2] See Adriaansz (1973) for an exhaustive discussion
of kumiuta.

[3] See Adriaansz (1973) for an exhaustive discussion
of danmono.

more traditional <u>koto</u> music to decline. The salvation
of the situation was seen by <u>koto</u> masters (particularly
Ikuta Kengyō, 1656-1716) to be the pairing of <u>koto</u> with
<u>shamisen</u>, and indeed that quickly became standard ensemble
practice in the Osaka-Kyoto region where Ikuta Kengyō's
tradition (Ikuta <u>ryū</u>) was strong. The music played in
<u>koto-shamisen</u> ensemble was based on previously existing
<u>shamisen</u> forms, particularly <u>jiuta</u> (Malm 1959: 169).
<u>Jiuta</u> was originally a term used to distinguish <u>shamisen</u>
music of Kyoto from that of Edo (Tokyo), but in the
eighteenth century it came to mean more: 1) <u>koto</u> and
<u>shamisen</u> ensemble with a third instrument, the bowed
<u>kokyū</u>, usually added (an ensemble called <u>sankyoku</u>
"three instruments"); 2) compositions alternating vocal
sections and instrumental interludes but with greater
emphasis on the instruments than in the previously
existing <u>shamisen</u> forms; 3) lyrical, non-narrative
texts with the flexible form of <u>shamisen</u>-accompanied
song (and therefore without the formal rigidity of <u>koto</u>
kumiuta).

　　　Composition of <u>jiuta</u> flourished throughout the
eighteenth and nineteenth centuries. The interludes
between song portions became of such length that they
were called <u>tegoto</u> rather than <u>ai-no-te</u> and the terms
referring to the song portions were oriented to the
<u>tegoto</u>. With two or three song sections the form
would be:

(a)　　<u>Mae-uta</u>　　　<u>Tegoto</u>　　　<u>Ato-uta</u>
　　　　Fore-song　　Instrumental　 After-song
　　　　　　　　　　　　　Portion

(b)　<u>Mae-uta</u>　<u>Tegoto</u>　<u>Naka-uta</u>　<u>Tegoto</u>　<u>Ato-uta</u>.
　　　　　　　　　　　　　Middle
　　　　　　　　　　　　　Song

Some scholars distinguish two types within jiuta--
tegotomono and utamono, depending on the emphasis
within the composition.[4]

At the end of the eighteenth century in Tokyo
another tradition of koto music was begun (Yamada ryū)
which stressed utamono with narrative texts. For a very
long time the only tegotomono performed by Yamada musicians were borrowed from the Ikuta tradition (Adriaansz
1973: 466).

In the nineteenth century antipathy developed in
the Ikuta ryū for the pairing of koto and shamisen in
ensemble, and compositions gradually appeared that
featured koto alone or two kotos together (honte and
kaede).[5] Emphasis on the instrument became ever more
important; most new compositions were for two kotos and
included only two song portions -- the mae-uta and ato-
uta. That is the type selected for study here.

In many tegotomono there are brief introductions
to the major sections and transitions between them, but
these are optional. In published koto scores they may
or may not be labelled as separate entities, but the

[4] This distinction is drawn by Adriaansz (1973:
466) in classifying the repertoire of classical sokyoku.
Malm did not draw the distinction in his 1959 book:
"The most important form of koto composition is the
jiuta. It is a hybrid form, combining the techniques
of both kumiuta and shirabemono. This music is sometimes called tegotomono, because its important contri-
bution to koto music is the use of tegoto, instrumental
interludes." (p. 181)

[5] In Japan the terms used for the two parts are
te-on and ko-on, but honte and kaede are used in the
literature in English.

listing below shows what they will be labelled if they
are. Internal subdivisions within <u>tegoto</u> sections are

	<u>Mae-biki</u>	Short <u>koto</u> introductory passage
I <u>Mae-uta</u>	<u>Mae-uta</u>	
	<u>Tsunagi</u>	<u>Koto</u> conclusion of <u>uta</u> section
	<u>Makura</u> (<u>jo</u>)	Introduction to <u>tegoto</u>
	<u>Mae-jirashi</u>	Further introduction or "fore-climax"
II <u>Tegoto</u>	<u>Tegoto</u>	
	<u>Naka-jirashi</u>	Mid-<u>tegoto</u> climax
	<u>Tegoto</u>	
	<u>Hon-jirashi</u>	Final climax or "true climax"
III <u>Ato-uta</u>	<u>Ato-uta</u>	
	<u>Ato-biki</u>[6]	Short closing <u>koto</u> passage

often labelled <u>dans</u>. In Chart 1 these various subsections are shown as they occur in the five <u>tegotomono</u>
chosen for this study: "Chidori," "Haru no Kyoku,"
"Saga no Aki," "Shin Takasago," and "Aki no Koto no Ha."
These particular pieces are performed in the Yamada as
well as in the Ikuta tradition.

The <u>mae-biki</u> and <u>mae-uta</u> begin at a stately, slow
speed. While the <u>tegoto</u> is begun slowly, the speed
accelerates gradually; at internal divisions -- the end
of a <u>dan</u>, for example-- there is usually a slight
ritardando, followed by renewed acceleration in the next

---

[6] <u>Ato-biki</u> is listed in Adriaansz 1973: 15. Many
<u>koto</u> teachers are not familiar with the term.

segment. The transition to the <u>ato-uta</u> is made by a
ritardando often reinforced by a decrease of rhythmic
density in the melody. The singer determines the
speed of the <u>ato-uta</u>; it usually moves slowly to allow
him or her to interpret the part effectively.

 This book on <u>tegotomono</u> is a revision of a thesis
for an M.A. degree in music: <u>A Selective Study of
Honte-Kaete Tegotomono in Nineteenth-Century Japanese
Koto Music</u> (UCLA 1967). For the purposes of the
thesis the five compositions mentioned above were
chosen because they span most of the nineteenth century
and because they reflect some of the changes in composition for a traditional instrument in a decisive
period of the history of music in Japan. In revising
the thesis the scope of the study was left intact. It
was not and is not meant to be a comprehensive coverage
of an enormous subject, but rather what its original
title suggested, a selective study. The approach to
the material has also remained basically the same, with
attention to cultural history, to text and text setting,
song and song accompaniment, <u>honte</u> and <u>kaede</u> <u>koto</u> parts.
However, the analysis of the material has been revised
to some extent and the presentation of the analysis to
a great extent. It is hoped that this study provides a
basic understanding of <u>tegotomono</u> and that the state-
ments made about the genre will be borne out in further
work on a much larger selection of compositions.

 A few nitty-gritty notes on procedure are in order.
In this study I have avoided use of musical terminology
loaded with connotations of the Western system of
functional harmony: "base pitch" is preferred to "tonic,"
"the pitch at the interval of a fifth from base pitch"

Chart 1: Structures of the Five Compositions

I Mae-uta	II Tegoto	III Ato-uta
Chidori Mae-biki Mae-uta Tsunagi not labelled Measure 71 n.l. (n.l.) 14	Ikuta ryū: "Section of Waves" "Section of Plovers" 79 103 Yamada ryū: Makura Mae-jirashi Tegoto 79 n.l. 90 n.l. 103	Ato-uta 154-199
Haru no Kyoku Mae-biki Mae-uta 6	Ikuta ryū: Tegoto Kaede begins Chirashi 114 162 308 Yamada ryū: Makura Mae-jirashi Dan I Dan II 114 137 162 n.l. 308 Kaede begins	Ato-uta 386-435
Saga no Aki Mae-uta 2	Ikuta ryū: Dan I Dan II Dan III 58 132 250 Yamada ryū: Dan I ritard Dan II Dan III 58 253 282	Ato-uta 374-401
Shin Takasago Mae-uta Tsunagi 2 39 n.l.	Tegoto 48	Ato-uta 133-141
Aki no Koto no Ha Mae-biki Mae-uta Tsunagi 11 105 n.l.	Tegoto Dan II (Tsunagi 105-112 n.l.) 90 105	Ato-uta 263-308

rather than "dominant," and the like. Interval desig-
nations such as minor third, major second from the
Western tempered tuning system have been utilized,
however, because most Japanese <u>koto</u> players now tune
their instruments to those intervals. It has even
become customary to use a Western tuning fork to get
a standardized starting pitch.

Complete transcriptions of the five compositions
made from published scores and one manuscript comprise
Appendix II. In the thesis the complete transcriptions
were from Ikuta scores, with differences in Yamada
editions shown for each piece. Since the greatest
number of discrepancies between the Ikuta and Yamada
scores are in "Chidori," the thesis format is retained
here for that one composition. For the other four only
the transcriptions from Ikuta scores are included. For
"Chidori," "Haru no Kyoku," "Aki no Koto no Ha," and
"Shin Takasago" **the** transcriptions have been revised
to conform to 1971 editions.

A large number of brief examples are sprinkled
throughout the text to demonstrate specific points.
The number in a box at the beginning of each example
is the measure number in the complete transcription;
in the text "m." is the abbreviation for "measure" and
"ms." for "measures." The Western five-line staff was
found to be suitable for transcription because the
intervals are the same size. Bar lines are placed as
they are placed in the Japanese scores. Accidentals
are notated at the beginning of each beat and remain
in effect through the beat unless a change is indicated.

Numbers (1-13) written above the staff line refer
to particular strings that are to be played, while the
numbers "2" or "3" below the staff and underneath particular pitches indicate that the index finger (2) or
middle finger (3) of the right hand is to be used for
playing; otherwise it is understood that the thumb is
used. Ikuta symbols for techniques are used throughout;
they are explained as they occur and also in Appendix I
which gives information on several Japanese notation
systems for koto music.

Today tegotomono occupies a cherished place as
one of the most vibrant genres of the koto tradition.
Tegotomono music, its poetry, and musicians who have
played it are part of Japan's rich cultural history,
and this is its story.

TEGOTOMONO
Music for the Japanese Koto

ONE / The Culture and the *Koto*

The earliest history of Japan is known only through
legend and archaeological evidence and finally emerges
in the matrices of myths and traditions so skillfully
woven into the Kojiki (Record of Ancient Matters,
712 A.D.) and Nihon Shoki (History of Japan, 720 A.D.).
These compilatory efforts to give a respectable and
ancient geneaology to the ruling family introduced the
Nara period of Japanese history.

From the eighth through the twelfth centuries, the
periods of Nara and Heian rule, cultural embassies were
sent to China from the tiny islands to learn and to
acquire those items deemed suitable for adaptation to
Japanese culture. The Japanese borrowed ideas of
government, styles of architecture, concepts of town
planning, and a further vital cultural element — a
system of writing. They also borrowed art forms and
musical instruments among which was the cheng, and
thus began the history of the koto.[1]

The cheng was a Chinese stringed instrument of the
zither type with moveable bridges. Elongated by the
Japanese and made slightly arched like the back of a

---

[1] For an excellent discussion of cultural borrowings
see Fairbank, Reischauer, and Craig (1973).

dragon, the instrument assumed a new, more elegant form and took its place among the instruments favored at the Japanese Imperial court.[2]

Coeval with these developments were further borrowings from the T'ang court in China of court rituals, ceremonies, dances, and music of the court orchestra, all vital to the general style of imperial life. Gagaku, the orchestral music developed in Japan from T'ang and Nara times, flourishes in the Japanese court today and is the oldest continuous orchestral music tradition in the world. Included in the ensemble is the gaku-sō (sō-no-koto), the form of the koto from which the history of the instrument in Japan can be traced.[3]

The Nara period (710-784) was one of technological and cultural growth under a centralized political system. Buddhist art, temples, and ethical value system penetrated and became absorbed into Japanese life. Calligraphy and literature which were so actively cultivated in China were pursued by the island elites, and forms and styles of Chinese literature were adapted to the Japanese language. From the Nara period dates the Manyōshū (A Collection of Myriad Leaves) containing 4516 poems, the majority of which are tanka, short poems of thirty-one syllables divided into lines of 5-7-5-7-7 syllables. The composition of tanka is still practiced today.

---

[2] One legendary account of the espousal of the instrument is given in Piggott (1909) 32-37. For historical data see Harich-Schneider (1973): Shō-sōin collection, seventh to first half of the eighth centuries, p. 64; ninth century, pp. 102, 146.

[3] See Malm (1959) Chapters 3 and 7.

Japan

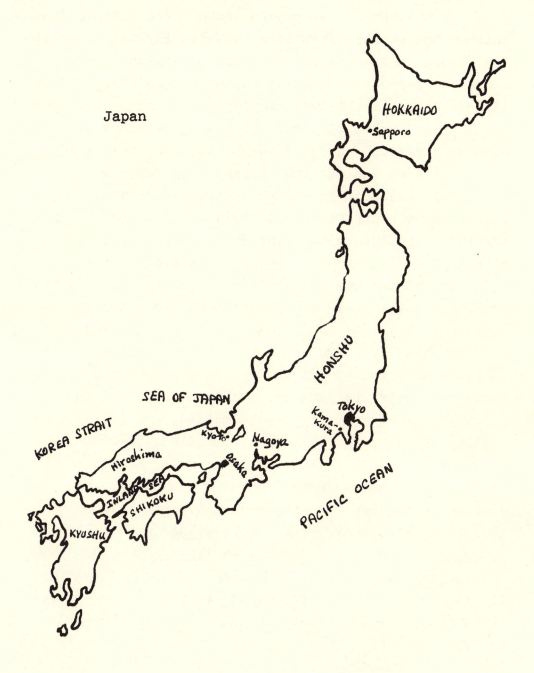

At the end of the eighth century the emperor Kammu shifted the capital from Nara to Heian (Kyoto) to escape the strong influences of the religious establishments, and a new period in Japanese history began (Heian 794-1185). Heian is the beginning of a traceable distinctive Japanese culture, secure in its adaptations of Chinese elements and confident of standing on its own in the wake of the decline of its T'ang mentor.

By the end of the ninth century one branch of one of the great court families, the Fujiwara, came to exert tremendous influence at court and in government, to the extent that "It gradually became accepted . . . that the emperors reigned but did not rule." (Fairbank, Reischauer, and Craig 1973: 351) The arts flourished under the Fujiwara. Use of a new form of writing which was half Chinese, half Japanese began to crowd the former total reliance on Chinese, and the emphasis at court on composition of poetry in Japanese increased. In 905 the second imperial anthology was compiled, the Kokinshū (Ancient and Modern Collection). While male writers of prose continued to employ Chinese, ladies at court who knew Japanese better than Chinese wrote novels and diaries which were the outstanding literary pieces of the day. Among these were a novel, The Tale of Lady Ochikubo, of the tenth century and The Tale of Genji (Genji Monogatari) by Lady Murasaki, a work of fiction but which is thought nevertheless to give a good picture of court life and of music in court life in the early eleventh century (Fairbank, Reischauer, and Craig 1973: 357). Performances on the koto were apparently frequent and a solo tradition flourished for which the literary references are the only documentation (Adriaansz 1973: 4).

The hegemony of the Fujiwara family did not endure. In Heian Japan control of the central government and even the power of the government's provincial representatives began to wane. A private proprietor estate system evolved which receded from the Chinese-style centralized bureaucracy to one of more familiar, personalized, decentralized political relationships. Religious institutions and noble families rather than a central government dominated a country which was in a period of tremendous economic and cultural growth.[4] The Japanese forms of economy, polity, and culture diffused from Kyoto throughout the islands. Although this is not possible to trace, it may have been as part of such diffusion that the tradition of <u>koto</u> music reached the southern island of Kyushu where it surfaced in documentary sources in the sixteenth century.

The enormous cultural and estate-economy growth of Heian Japan gave impetus to a provincial warrior group who were needed to protect the large estates against marauding bandits. Eventually these groups of military guards emerged as a powerful warrior aristocracy, the <u>bushi</u> ("warrior") or <u>samurai</u> ("retainer") class. Where there are bands of warriors, it seems there will be competition, and the tenth and eleventh centuries on the main island of Honshu indeed were marked by armed

---

[4] Fairbank, Reischauer, and Craig say that there was gradual disintegration of institutions of the central government and decline in law and order from the tenth to the twelfth centuries. But contrary to writings which noted an aura of decay and catastrophe, these centuries were in fact a period of great economic and cultural growth (1973: 352-53).

strife between two branches of one samurai clan: the
Minamoto (or Genji) and Taira (or Heike). The struggle
became increasingly important to the "nation" when it
came to focus on the capital, Kyoto, and it was realized
how dominant the power of the military had become.

   In 1185 the Minamoto triumphed over the Taira and
a new form of feudal power was established. While the
imperial family continued to live and reign in Kyoto,
the real power was based in the military and at a sea-
side town, Kamakura, close to present-day Tokyo. His-
torians have labelled the period from 1185-1333 the
Kamakura Shogunate. In essence it was a period in which
political, economic, and military authority were one and
the same, defined in terms of property rights and feudal
relationships. In effect the system endured until the
Meiji Restoration in the nineteenth century. The climate
of war, with its prime virtues of loyalty and duty, led
to the composition of tales even of epic length such as
the Heike Monogatari which were often chanted in court
and for the populace to the accompaniment of a lute
(biwa).

   Through the Kamakura Shogunate and particularly in
the following period of the Ashikaga Shogunate (1333-
1573) economic and cultural activity flourished. Land-
scape architecture and art, prose and poetry proliferated
aesthetically dominated by Zen Buddhist values. The Nō
drama, which evolved from symbolic court dances and more
popular mime and other dramatic traditions, became in
the fourteenth century a full-fledged theatrical form
which captivated the patronage of the samurai aristocracy.

The shift again to local concentration of power
within a feudal framework describes the situation at
the end of the Ashikaga Shogunate and into the sixteenth
century. Constant warfare raged all over Japan for control of the land, and local military leaders began to
be true territorial lords (daimyo) in complete control
of well defined areas and populations. Amidst the wars
the economy boomed, cash crops were grown as well as
subsistence crops, local markets proliferated and trade
towns gradually appeared at ports which catered to
international trade or around religious institutions.
Currency began to replace barter, and merchant groups
became a viable segment of the population. Merchants
fell increasingly under the control of the daimyo,
however, and were compelled to serve the needs of the
government, "thus setting the pattern of political
control over economic activities that has remained
characteristic of Japan ever since." (Fairbank, Reischauer, and Craig 1973: 382)

In contrast to such an atmosphere of activity, a
quieter world existed in some places in Japan. In
Kyushu, koto music was taken into the serene sphere of
Buddhist and Confucian priests and of noblemen, removed
from the popular sphere. A tradition cultivated by a
priest musician, Kenjun (1547-1636), which derived from
gagaku, from Chinese ch'in music, and from temple tradition, was performed in the temples, but never for
popular entertainment. Kenjun's vocal-instrumental
compositions, called kumiuta, reflected the calm,
meditative mood of the atmosphere in which they were
composed. These, with a number of pieces selected from
a local tradition (zokkyoku) formed the repertoire of

what came to be called Tsukushi-goto and later, Tsukushi
ryū (Adriaansz 1973: 5).

By late sixteenth century the daimyo domains were
being used to build a relatively uniform and solid
national political structure. When Portuguese traders
and missionaries arrived in the 1540s and then within
two decades had begun to exert a noticeable influence on
local populations, a movement was spurred which ended
ultimately in the expulsion of the foreigners, isolation
of Japan from other Asian cultures, and a forceful
national unification under the Tokugawa Shogunate, centered at Edo (Tōkyo).

From about 1600 until mid-nineteenth century, the
Tokugawa political organization resulted in a substan-
tial period of political stability, urban growth,
continued commercial expansion, and the development of
two strong cultural traditions, one dominated by the
warrior class and the other by city-dwellers. The nation
was ruled through a tightly controlled coalition of
ostensibly autonomous daimyo which was never centralized.
Social mobility came to a practical standstill. Classes
were frozen by law, preventing military retainers from
leaving the service of their lords to become merchants
or farmers, and vice versa. There was a clear line
between samurai and commoners, but the demarkations were
fuzzy below that. Artisans and merchants were ranked
about the same, classified chōnin, townsmen.

Even within an atmosphere of such strict control,
literature, art, music, and the theater flowered. In
the thriving urban context publishing houses catered to
a new widespread literacy, using woodblock printing
rather than moveable type to permit inclusion of

illustrations. New types of literature were developed, such as the short stories of Saikaku (1642-1693) in Osaka and the seventeen-syllable poetic form, haiku, which became a craze among all classes.

The samurai continued to support the Nō drama, but the chōnin preferred new theatrical forms such as jōruri, the puppet theater that brought into widespread popularity the shamisen, a three-stringed spiked lute that the narrator used for accompaniment. Another popular theater that had developed early in the seventeenth century, kabuki, had featured performances by men and women, but prostitution had become associated with it, so women had been banned from the stage. Kabuki did not successfully compete with joruri until the eighteenth century.

The merchants in the cities were hardworking, disciplined people with a goal-oriented rather than status-oriented ethic. But they were wealthy, and in search of fashion and entertainment. Diversion was for men and to be sought outside of the home since home meant money-making and family, and thus the pleasure quarters of the cities grew. They became the centers of social life and aesthetic activity and provided relief from the rigidity of the Tokugawa order. In the pleasure quarters the more beautiful and skilled women became courtesans, taught to sing dance, and entertain. The favored musical instrument was the shamisen, which they played to accompany numerous types of song. This, plus the reliance on shamisen in the burgeoning theatrical sphere assured its place as the most widely appreciated instrument of the time.

The popular entertainment world and the type of songs accompanied on the shamisen were the antithesis of

the more formal world in which the <u>koto</u> and its music
were being cultivated. Under Genjō (d. 1662), Kenjun's
student and successor as head of the tradition, the
sphere of performance of Tsukushi <u>ryū</u> was restricted
even further. No longer was the <u>koto</u> to be taught to
blind men who transmitted more popular traditions; nor
was it to be played by women (Adriaansz 1973: 6). Only
in violation of such strict regulations was it likely
that the Tsukushi <u>ryū</u> could have any influence on the
mainstream of musical culture.

And that proved to be the case. Genjō's student,
Hōsui, who was sent to perform in Kyoto, was not favor-
ably received there for reasons unknown to us. He left
Kyoto for Edo where he defied the dictates of his <u>ryū</u>
and taught a limited number of Tsukushi-goto pieces to
a blind <u>shamisen</u> player. While Hōsui was expelled from
his tradition, the <u>shamisen</u> player he taught moved to
Kyoto and became one of the most famous composers in
the history of <u>koto</u> music, Yatsuhashi Kengyō (1614-1685).[5]
Yatsuhashi changed the tuning of several Tsukushi-goto
<u>kumiuta</u> and composed new ones. While <u>kumiuta</u> to a
<u>shamisen</u> player usually meant a set of short songs with
intimate, romantic texts and certainly no fixed form,
Yatsuhashi's compositions reflected the <u>koto</u> tradition
he had learned: the texts were taken from classical

---

[5] For a more detailed discussion see Adriaansz
(1973) 7. Adriaansz disputes a frequently related
version of this story, that Yatsuhashi went to Kyushu
to study with Genjō. That version is related in
Harich-Schneider (1973) 519. <u>Kengyō</u> was the highest
title awarded to blind male musicians.

literary sources and the songs were in strict form.[6]

While Yatsuhashi Kengyō succeeded in moving koto music into a more popular sphere than the one in which it had existed, he did not change the musical tide of the times. With the ascendancy of the shamisen in the entertainment world of the new urban centers, solo koto music was in danger of being lost in the cultural shuffle. Ikuta Kengyō (1666-1716), a second generation successor of Yatsuhashi Kengyō, realized that music for the koto had best follow the mainstream. He respectfully waited until both Yatsuhashi and his own teacher died before established a new school of koto music, the Ikuta ryū (from 1698). Ikuta encouraged his students to turn to shamisen for new ideas and to perform in ensemble with shamisen. His advice was followed to the extent that for more than 100 years after the founding of the ryū the koto was so dependent on shamisen that only scattered compositions were written for solo koto. The music which the two instruments shared in ensemble was not of the licentious entertainment quarter ilk, however; while a bit livelier in mood than koto kumiuta, it was still formal and refined.

From the days of Yatsuhashi Kengyō koto playing was opened to persons other than priests and noblemen. Professional blind musicians (male) composed and performed, but what is important is that young girls of well-to-do families sought and were taught koto lessons. They were not permitted to perform professionally, but

---

[6] For more detail on shamisen kumiuta, see Adriaansz (1973) 9-10.

it was a gentlewomanly grace to be able to play.

Through the eighteenth century, then, koto and shamisen provided dignified musical entertainment in homes in the Osaka-Kyoto area. In Edo (Tōkyo) where the Shogun resided, the tastes of the populace were apparently different. One the whole they were unattracted to traditional culture including koto music, and the song styles which they preferred were narrative rather than lyrical. Ikuta ryū musicians found that lamentable and sent Nasetomi Kengyō from Kyoto to spread traditional Ikuta koto music. He was welcomed in Edo by Yamada Shōboku, a doctor who had previously studied Ikuta kumikyoku with Mitsuhashi Kengyō (d. 1760), the last great composer of kumiuta masterpieces. The doctor soon became the student of his guest.[7]

In Edo was a young man, Mita Ryogin (1757-1817), who had moved to the capital from his birthplace in Mikawa, Shizuoka Prefecture. The son of a Nō actor of the Hōshō school, Ryogin had became blind in his youth and turned to the only profession other than music that was open to the blind--that of masseur. Each time he went to a shrine to pray he paused outside the house of a teacher of kato-bushi (a narrative song genre) to listen and to study the playing. After composing one piece in the kato-bushi style, Ryogin went to a public bath, as the story goes, and sang it for the people to see their reaction. If they praised it, he thought he would complete the song and sing it publicly as it was his ambition to sing for all people, not only the

[7] Information on Yamada ryū from Fujita Reiro (1923) 469-72. No dates available for Nasetomi Kengyō or Yamada Shōboku.

wealthy. The fame of Mita Ryogin spread from the public
bath through the populace to the higher classes. He was
soon invited to perform for the warrior class, the top
level of Edo society.

In time Mita Ryogin became the <u>koto</u> student of
Yamada Shōbuku, then his disciple of the "first rank,"
and finally he took his teacher's professional name,
Yamada, to become Yamada Kengyō. A musician reputedly
sensitive to his time and to the people around him, he
was attentive to the styles of music that they liked and
ingested them into his music for the <u>koto</u>, uninterested
in monetary returns but very interested in being close to
people and in creating art. He was said to be typical of
the Edo personality--witty, generous, not concerned with
what the next day would bring.[8]

The attempt by Ikuta musicians to spread their
tradition in Edo was unsuccessful because Yamada Kengyō
established a new school, Yamada <u>ryū</u>, that catered to
Edo tastes. <u>Katō-bushi</u>, <u>itchū-bushi</u>, and <u>tomimoto-bushi</u>
from which he drew his inspiration and ideas were of the
narrative genre of <u>shamisen</u> music, <u>katarimono</u> (Malm 1959:
188-203). Also included in his sources were the music of
the Nō drama--probably due to his father's profession and
to the popularity of the Nō theater among the <u>samurai</u>--
and the chanting of epic poetry such as the <u>Heike Monoga-
tari</u> to <u>biwa</u> accompaniment. The stress on the narrative
gave greater importance to the song than to the <u>koto</u>, and

[8] This description of the Tokyo personality was also
expressed to me by a <u>koto</u> teacher in Los Angeles, Kazue
Kudo, a native Japanese. She insisted the personality
makes a difference in the music of the Yamada style.

that is the distinction most often quoted as a major
difference between the Ikuta and Yamada styles.[9] Quite
contrary to the Edo love of showiness, however, Yamada
Kengyō discarded the paint and the decorative tassels
on the Ikuta instruments, leaving bare the beautiful
grain of the wood.[10]

Throughout the Tokugawa era the country was
governed by a feudal aristocracy dependent on an agrarian
base of support. But the new urban culture had become so
economically successful that the warrior echelon of society found themselves increasingly impoverished and in-
debted to the lower-ranking merchants. For various
reasons morale declined among the samurai who had not
been called upon to act as warriors in one of the longest
periods of peace Japan had ever known.

In the eighteenth century interest was again shown
in Europe, and especially in its technology. In 1720
the shogunate relaxed its ban on Western books except for
those concerning Christianity, and scholars began to go
to the Dutch trading port at Nagasaki to study "Dutch
learning," as all study of Western subjects was categorized.

Through the eighteenth and into the nineteenth century a series of reforms were tried by successive shoguns;
some were successful, some not. Most recent scholarship
maintains that although there were serious socio-economic

[9] It is a legitimate difference for the music of
the nineteenth century, but with later developments,
the koto received its fair share of attention by
Yamada musicians.

[10] For more detail on changes in the instrument,
see Adriaansz (1973) Chapter 2.

difficulties through that period, in 1850 "the <u>samurai</u>
Confucian ethic still pervaded the nation, and the whole
Tokugawa political structure still stood firm. If Japan
had continued free of foreign encroachment, the Tokugawa
system might well have continued for quite some time
longer without major change." (Fairbank, Reischauer, and
Craig 1973: 434)

The Russians were the first to exert pressure on
Japan in the nineteenth century, then the British. By
mid-nineteenth century the United States had become the
nation most interested in opening the country. The
success of the American naval envoys in 1854 opened a
Pandora's box of ills for the shogunate in more than the
obvious ways. Discussion was opened to all of the <u>daimyo</u>
for the first time in two and a half centuries of shogunate rule and discontent with many internal affairs came
pouring forth (Fairbank, Reischauer, and Craig 1973: 487).

The years between 1853 when a decisive American
envoy sailed into Edo Bay and 1868 when the rule of the
shogunate ended were filled with complex machinations and
decision-making. The sanction of the Emperor was increasingly sought for whatever action was to be taken, and
ultimately the change in government was couched in terms
of an "imperial restoration." In 1868 young Emperor
Meiji became symbolically the head of the nation and the
imperial capital was moved to Edo which was renamed Tokyo,
the "Eastern Capital." The new government was formed
primarily from the <u>samurai</u> who had led the final assault
on the Tokugawa forces, and Japan proceeded with moderni-
zation along Western lines.

The tenor of the nation in the Meiji Restoration
period was one of national pride, faith in the future,

and moralistic fervor. To a few composers of songs in
koto music this meant rewriting texts from lyric,
romantic to educational, even patriotic. But the change
of government affected the musical world in a much more
serious and potentially disruptive manner. When in the
Meiji Reforms the institutions of a feudal state were
being dismantled, the powerful guild of blind musicians,
the Shoku-Yashiki, was also disbanded. The effect of
this on koto music cannot be overestimated, for the whole
hierarchy of professional musicians, the monopoly of the
blind master, was no longer legal. Their special privi-
leges and rankings were gone so that none again would
bear the title kengyō. But gone too were the imposing
obligations and restrictions. Those individuals able to
meet the competitive musical world on their own realized
that the koto as a household instrument could be better
adapted to the new government policies than the shamisen
which was so inextricably bound to the popular entertainment world (Toyotaka 1956: 347). Through the composition of koto tegotomono and the disassociation from
shamisen in performance the koto was returned to its
place of prominence.

For those players who wanted to continue the koto-
shamisen ensemble tradition that had become so securely
entrenched in the Tokugawa era, there was still sankyoku,
the ensemble of koto, shamisen, and now the shakuhachi,
a vertical bamboo flute which displaced the bowed kokyū.
Musically the roles are reversed, however, for the koto
is the lead instrument with the other two parts modeled
on the contour of its melody.

At the end of the nineteenth century interest
surged in the publication of koto scores and in new

playing techniques. From that point in the history of
koto music to the present day there has been a stream of
experimentation and innovation. Seventeen-string kotos
and even larger instruments have been developed and
compositions written for them; new ensemble combinations
have been tried including koto with chorus, and koto with
Western instruments.

All the while, the traditional music is taught,
learned, and heard in dignified contexts. Men and a few
women perform professionally and daughters of middle-
and upper-class families study koto as a gentlewomanly
pursuit. The sounds of [Genji's] zithern are one of the
beautiful reminders of an older Japan, away from the
rushing crowds and noises of congested cities. Behind
modern facades Japanese still keep a ritual, enjoying the
scent of blossoming trees, imbibing tea, and listening
to the sounds of the koto.

Both hands are needed to play the <u>koto</u>, but with
the exception of one technique the right hand strikes
the strings to play melody. More particularly, three
fingers of the right hand are used and picks are worn
on them: the thumb, the index and middle fingers. The
picks consist of two pieces: an ivory or plastic "nail"
(<u>tsume</u>) that fits into a ring (<u>wa</u>) made of layers of
thick paper and coated on the outside with a sealer such
as lacquer. The <u>tsume</u> is inserted down into a slit in
the ring and glued into place. The <u>tsume</u> and <u>wa</u> both
come in an assortment of sizes to accommodate different
players' finger sizes, because the pick must fit snugly
just above the top joint of those fingers, with the
"nail" extending beyond the fingers to the palm side of
the hand.

In the Ikuta tradition the <u>tsume</u> are square at the
end rather than rounded as in the older fashion. Ikuta
Kengyō is said to have changed their shape to facilitate
the playing of the adopted <u>shamisen</u> techniques, particularly the backstroke (<u>sukuizume</u>). Yamada Kengyō, on the
other hand, preferred the rounded shape and accordingly,
the two traditions use differently shaped picks.

A player sits at the far right end of the instrument to be situated conveniently at the playing area 1½ to 2 inches in from that end. Ikuta musicians follow another innovation by Ikuta Kengyo̅ and sit at an acute angle to the instrument, while Yamada musicians keep to their "founder's" preference for sitting straight on, at a right angle to the instrument. Traditionally the koto has been played resting on the tatami-mat floor and the player with legs tucked under sitting on a small pillow. As more Japanese homes have Western furnishings and fewer koto students find it comfortable to sit on their legs, it has become acceptable to rest the koto on a stand and sit in a chair to play. The aesthetic effect of the modern practice is far different from the traditional.

The right thumb is the busiest playing finger; if there is no indication in a score that the index (notated 2) or middle (3) finger is to be used, then it is assumed that the thumb will be used to produce the pitch. Techniques employing the index and middle fingers are numerous and for the most part idiomatic to the koto. Most serve to prolong a particular motive, or shift the pitch register from high to low or low to high; those techniques are referred to here as technical patterns because they produce a vocabulary of melodic and rhythmic patterns that are a vital element in the melodic process of this style of music. The left hand is used to embellish pitches in the melody and augment the repertoire of pitches available in the tuning. There are also techniques for both hands which modify the sound produced by a vibrating string. All of these techniques and the patterns they produce are discussed in the first section of this chapter.

Techniques and Technical Patterns

The techniques and technical patterns for the
right hand which occur in these compositions are listed
below and are demonstrated in Chart 2.[1]
Right Hand

1. Sukuizume--a backstroke with the tsume of the
thumb on a single string. This technique was borrowed
from the shamisen and thus became widely used from the
eighteenth century. On the koto it makes a lighter
sound than striking the string produces and also a
slightly scraping sound.

2. Awasezume-- two strings, in most instances in
these compositions an octave apart, struck simultaneously with thumb and middle finger.

3. Kakite--two adjacent strings struck with
thumb, index finger, or middle finger in a succession so
rapid that they seem simultaneous.

4. Oshiawase--two adjacent strings struck in
rapid succession with the thumb, while the lower pitched
of the two strings is pressed down by the left hand far
enough to raise its pitch to that of the higher, sounding
a unison.

5. Uraren or sararin--a downward glissando with
the picks of the index and middle fingers fluttering
from the thirteenth string to a specified lower one that
is struck with the thumb. This technique is begun
differently in the Ikuta and Yamada traditions, but the
pattern produced is similar.

[1] For a complete explanation of the techniques,
see Adriaansz (1973) Chapter 5.

Chart 2:   Right Hand Techniques and Technical Patterns

Hirajōshi Tuning

Sukuizume   Awasezume   Kakite   Oshiawase   Uraren

Hikiren   Hikisute   Nagashizume   Chirashizume

Surizume   Warizume   Kakezume

Extended kakezume   Hayakake

Unnamed technical patterns

6. Hikiren--an upward glissando with the middle
finger over all the strings, with the first two and
last two or three distinct. In the Ikuta style, the
middle of the glissando is barely audible.

7. Hikisute--a form of hikiren that does not
cover all the strings.

8. Nagashizume or kararin--a downward glissando
with the thumb from string thirteen to the lowest two
pitches which are heard distinctly.

9. Chirashizume--a fast, light movement with the
edge of the pick on the middle finger along one or two
strings from right to left, resulting in a swishing
sound.

10. Surizume--strings 5 and 6 scraped by the edge
of the picks of the index and middle fingers, from right
to left, and on the beat indicated, back to the right.
The desired effect is a scraping sound rather than
melodic pitch.

11. Warizume--two adjacent strings plucked almost
simultaneously by the index and middle fingers in turn.
Warizume is usually followed by the octave of the lower
of the two pitches hit together.

12. Kakezume--a melodic pattern adapted from
related patterns in gagaku, with the index and middle
fingers striking adjacent strings followed by the
octave of the lowest pitch. Variations of the kakezume
and an extended form are shown on Chart 2.

13. Hayakake--a "fast" (haya) kake. The melodic
patterns are similar to kakezume, but have shorter note-
values.

14. Three other techniques for the right hand
that are not named are also shown on Chart 2.

Warizume, kakezume, hayakake, and other patterns
which resolve to a higher octave of their lowest pitch
generally serve to prolong a moment in the progress of
the melody. This is demonstrated in Example 1; the
skeleton melody is notated below the full passage.
Note also the sukuizume in m. 116.

Example 1

Chidori tegoto honte

Sukuizume is used very often in these compositions, particularly in tegoto sections where melodic
alternation between honte and kaede (kakeai) occurs.
Awasezume come at climactic moments, such as the beginning and end of a section of the composition, or of a
single segment.

The glissando techniques are used especially in
tegoto, usually in both honte and kaede parts. Only
one-third as many occur in the song portions of tegotomono where the koto accompaniment is kept simple. When
they do occur in uta, they come either in the ai-no-te
or, more often, at the beginning or end of a new word

or phrase of text. In <u>honte</u> parts a good majority of
them are followed immediately by another technical
pattern such as <u>awase</u> or <u>warizume</u>, but this is not the
case in <u>kaede</u> parts.

In "Chidori" and "Haru no Kyoku" the greatest
number of the glissandos do not come to rest on one of
the primary tones of the tuning. In the later compositions, however, the primary tones would seen to be
emphasized by glissandos, for in "Saga no Aki" all
glissandos rest on one of the primary tones while in
"Shin Takasago" and "Aki no Koto no Ha" most of them do.

The scraping techniques appear in <u>honte</u> parts only
in <u>uta</u> portions of these compositions, but they appear
in the <u>tegoto</u> in <u>kaede</u> parts. As demonstrated in
Example 2 from the "Chidori" Ikuta score, the occasions
when the two-string version of <u>chirashizume</u> is called
for it appears more than once; in these pieces the
single-string version is always a single event. Both
types of <u>chirashizume</u> tend to appear on weak beats of
a measure, and are generally given the value of one or
one and a half beats.

Example 2

Chidori <u>mae-uta</u> <u>honte</u>   <u>tegoto</u> <u>kaede</u>

With only two exceptions in these compositions,
the <u>surizume</u> technique comes in <u>tegoto</u>, usually toward

or at the end of that section. Each of the movements
in the pair (right to left and left to right) has the
value of two or four beats, accentuating the feeling of
finality at that point, as demonstrated in Example 3.

Example 3

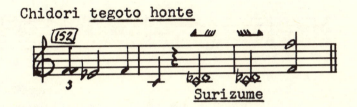

Chidori tegoto honte

Surizume

The techniques for the left hand involve the
raising and lowering of the pitch to which a string is
tuned. With the exception of the last listed below,
these techniques are applied to the portion of a string
to the left of the moveable bridge.

Left Hand

  1. Ko or oshide--pressing on the string to the
left of the bridge to obtain a pitch higher by a half-
step (♪), a whole step (♪), or occasionally a step and
a half (♪). The right hand then strikes the string.

  2. Oshi-hanashi--releasing an oshi-ed string,
letting the pitch lower to that of the open string while
the string still vibrates.

  3. Ēn or ato-oshi--raising of the pitch after an
open string has been struck and while the string still
vibrates.

  4. Kasaneoshi--prolongation of an ato-oshi by
releasing and re-raising the pitch.

5. <u>Chitsu</u> or <u>tsuki-iro</u>--the pitch of a vibrating string raised by an <u>ato-oshi</u> and lowered again quickly. Techniques 1-5 are shown in Example 4.

Example 4

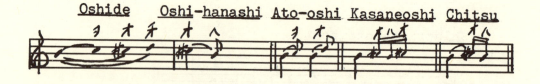

6. <u>Hiki-iro</u>--taking a vibrating string between the thumb and index fingers and pushing it toward the bridge gently to lower the pitch slightly, then releasing to raise it again to the original pitch. The effect is similar to that of the <u>kasaneoshi</u>, but done on an open string.

7. <u>Yogin</u> or <u>yuri-iro</u>--after striking a pitch a vibrato made by touching the string lightly with index and middle fingers.

8. <u>Keshizume</u>--lightly touching a vibrating string just under the string to the right of the bridge with the nail of the index finger to create a metallic sound. Indicated by " in notation.

The first of the techniques listed for the left hand, <u>oshide</u>, is the one most frequently called for in <u>koto</u> playing because it is not an ornamental technique in itself, but rather provides a way to fill the gaps in the tuning and expand the repertoire of pitches available. This technique is discussed in detail in the following chapter, since the use of it and the particular pitches produced by means of it are related specifically to the tunings. See pages 48-49.

Oshi-hanashi often appear doubled and even tripled, so that the pitch of a string is raised and lowered three times, ending on the open string pitch. In honte parts there are more oshi-hanashi; in kaede parts more kasaneoshi. Oshi-hanashi and kasaneoshi occur mostly in the uta portions of pieces in the honte, and in tegoto in the kaede parts. With two exceptions they all fall on the primary pitches of the tunings. In the kokingumi and in "Aki no Koto no Ha," one of these techniques ornaments the flatted leading tone which precedes the very ends of the compositions.

Ato-oshi are employed for melodic-rhythmic embellishment and also as integral to a basic melodic line. They occur through the compositions, though each piece has a preponderance of them in one portion or another. For example, in "Saga no Aki" and in "Haru no Kyoku" they are important in the tegoto section; "Shin Takasago" and "Aki no Koto no Ha" have relatively more in the combined uta accompaniments than in the tegoto. No general pattern is discernable for the distribution of ato-oshi in honte or kaede parts.

Ato-oshi are a means of melodic and rhythmic embellishment when appended to pitches of short duration, for they pass by very quickly and are usually on weak portions of beats. (See Example 5.) When of longer duration and particularly when they fall on the strong part of a beat, they are a more obvious part of a melodic line. They can create melodic repetition and anticipation as in Example 5(a) and (b). As demonstrated

in Example 5(c) a favorite use of <u>ato-oshi</u> is to obtain
an upper neighbor tone, often emphasizing the interval
of the tritone.

Example 5

(a) Saga no Aki   <u>tegoto</u> <u>kaede</u>

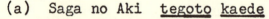
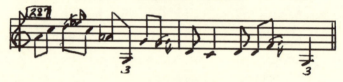

(b) Shin Takasago / Saga no Aki
        <u>honte</u>   <u>honte</u>

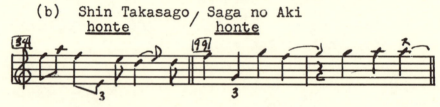

(c) Aki no Koto no Ha   <u>tegoto</u>

<u>Ato-oshi</u> are normally given half the value of the
pitches to which they are appended. Exceptions to this,
such as the pitch being changed either immediately after
the base note has been struck, or just before the next
pitch, are a matter of performance style.

Left hand techniques other than <u>oshide</u> provide
means for subtle interpretation of a melody. In the
transcriptions of the five compositions in this study
the embellishments are notated as in printed scores, but

their placement and number are subject to considerable flexibility in performance.

Tsuki-iro and yuri-iro are two techniques most often left to a performer to insert as he wishes. Tsuki-iro are used frequently and in all parts of compositions. They are particularly numerous in the notated honte parts of "Saga no Aki" and "Haru no Kyoku." Yuri-iro are notated in the song portions of "Chidori" and "Aki no Koto no Ha," but not the vibrato technique mentioned here; those yuri call for a quick release of an oshide and are in effect a fast version of oshi-hanashi.

Hiki-iro is one of the most frequently used of these techniques. It is notated in greatest number in the honte parts of "Chidori" (mae-uta only) and in "Saga no Aki" (thirty-four in this alone). None are notated in the scores of the other pieces, and none in the kaede of "Chidori." Their absence in notation is not an indication that they are not used, however; it is confirmation of their interpretive role.

The keshizume technique most always occurs with a syncopated rhythmic motive. In "Saga no Aki," "Shin Takasago," and "Aki no Koto no Ha" it occurs in the middle of the tegoto sections, but in "Chidori," "Haru no Kyoku," and "Saga no Aki," it appears notated near the ends of the tegoto. In all the pieces but "Shin Takasago" keshizume fall on primary tuning pitches.

Summary

Only the glissando techniques and the oshi-hanashi and kasaneoshi occur mostly in uta sections; sukuizume,

surizume, keshizume, and left-hand plucking come in
the tegoto sections, The remainder are distributed
about equally throughout compositions.

Many of these techniques emphasize the primary
pitches of the tunings, but the ones which are the most
interpretive often fall on pitches other than these as
well. Awasezume, oshiawase, and kakite serve to emphasize single pitches, while the glissando techniques give
a sweeping view of several of them. Ato-oshi, kasaneoshi,
oshi-hanashi, chitsu, hiki-iro, yuri-iro, keshizume, and
the scraping techniques embellish the tuning pitches by
adding complementary pitches or a special sound. Only
oshide which adds other pitches does not in some way
reiterate the tuning.

In the next chapter the tunings to which the koto
can be set are discussed. Since particular tunings are
used for particular compositions, the chapter begins with
a brief discussion of the five compositions that are
considered in this study.

THREE

The Compositions in the Study

Histories

It is difficult to know precisely when and sometimes precisely by whom tegotomono were composed. More than one musician often contributed to a piece when, for example, a previously existing tegoto was combined with new uta, or when a tegoto section was inserted into an utamono. One musician frequently composed a piece while another arranged it for different performing ensemble; or one man wrote a tegoto honte and another wrote a kaede for the honte (or even several different musicians wrote kaede for that honte). The histories of the compositions in this study are therefore difficult to document, and the sketches given below are open to dispute.

"Chidori." Sources agree at least that Yoshizawa Kengyō composed the uta and tegoto honte of "Chidori." According to The History of the Tsuyama School, "Chidori" was composed around the beginning of the Meiji period (1868-1912) after the example set by Mitsuzaka Kengyō of Kyoto (d. 1853) of writing a piece for koto without shamisen (1932: 455-56).

Mitsuzaki Kengyō who played both shamisen and koto apparently composed for both instruments. In fact, he

is cited as one of the leading composers in the Tempō
Period (1830-1843) when the music for shamisen-koto
ensemble was at its height but when the reaction against
it had begun to set in (Adriaansz 1973: 16). Mitsuzaki
Kengyō thus bridged two periods in the history of koto
composition and excelled in both. His "Godan Ginuta"
for two kotos and "Akikaze no Kyoku" for solo koto have
been heralded as masterpieces and setters of precedent.
"Akikaze" in particular is said to have influenced
Yoshizawa Kengyō, for "Akikaze" was composed on the model
of traditional sōkyoku combining six dans for instrumental solo and six uta in the fashion of danmono and
kumiuta (however loosely constructed) and "Chidori" also
included elements of traditional sōkyoku. "Chidori"
appears then to have been composed sometime between the
Tempō Period and early Meiji. According to one source
"it is said" that "Chidori" was composed first for
kokyū, then arranged for koto to be played with kokyū
(Fujita 1934: 21).

The element of traditional sōkyoku in "Chidori" is
not form, but song text. The form is that of shamisen-
related tegotomono (uta--tegoto--uta), but the uta texts
are poems from the tenth-century imperial anthology, the
Kokinshū. Unlike jiuta texts, they were formal in
structure and mood, having been written by strict rules
and in the dignified context of the court.

"Haru no Kyoku." The texts for four other compositions by Yoshizawa Kengyō were also from the Kokinshū,
and for that reason these pieces are referred to as the
five kokingumi: "Haru no Kyoku ("Composition for
Spring"), "Natsu no Kyoku" ("Summer"), "Aki no Kyoku"
("Autumn"), "Tsuyu [Fuyu] no Kyoku" ("Winter"), and
"Chidori no Kyoku" ("The Sea Plovers"). Unlike "Chidori"

the four on the subject of the seasons were not in
tegotomono form; rather they were a series of six songs
after the fashion of kumiuta. But as in "Akikaze" the
structures of the six songs were not the formalized
structure of traditional koto kumiuta. Thus the idea
was traditional while the carrying out of the idea was
contemporary.

However contemporary the song form was, the time
had apparently passed when musical audiences would be
content with compositions that neglected instrumental
portions (tegoto). The four seasonal kokingumi did not
become popular until late nineteenth century (mid-Meiji)
when another composer, Matsuzaka Harue of Kyoto (1854-
1920) added tegoto to them (Adriaansz 1973: 17).[1] Of
the kokingumi "Chidori," "Haru no Kyoku," and "Aki no
Kyoku" have been published in both Ikuta and Yamada
score and are often performed by musicians of both
schools. The two remaining kokingumi, "Natsu no Kyoku"
and "Fuyu no Kyoku," are reputedly shared but are performed less frequently and have been published only in
Ikuta score.

"Saga no Aki." "Saga no Aki" was composed by
Kikusue Kengyo of Osaka where a new style of "koto music"
was being developed; the new style focused on the song
texts, however. A group of Osaka musicians formed an

---

[1] This composer is listed as Matsuzaka Kengyo in
Fujita, Tonan (1932) 461 and as Matsuzaka Shungei in
Fujita (1934) 11. He might have held the rank kengyo
early in Meiji, but had to drop the title when the
Shoko-Yashiki was disbanded.

association to write <u>koto</u> songs more in keeping with the
reformist mood of early Meiji. Songs with educational
or patriotic texts, called "improved songs" (<u>kairyoshōka</u>),
were preferred to those on love and geisha life. At
first new songs were combined with old <u>tegoto</u>. For
example, Kikutaka Kengyō took the "Shōchikubai" <u>tegoto</u>,
wrote new <u>uta</u> and called the "improved" composition
"Kane no Naruki." Kikue Kengyō also took the "Shōchikubai" <u>tegoto</u> for his "Kiku no Asa," likewise the <u>tegoto</u>
of "Yūgao" for "Kusue no Ki no Tsuyu."[2] "Saga no Aki"
was one of the few <u>koto</u> pieces of that period to be
newly composed from beginning to end and was considered
a masterpiece among compositions at the beginning of the
Meiji era.

Although songs on romantic love were not considered
appropriate in the social and political reform era of the
imperial restoration, the text of "Saga no Aki" does
concern love. But it is love on a lofty plane and in an
imperial context, for it refers to an episode in the <u>Heike
Monogatari</u> which relates a search for Kogo no Tsubone, the
Emperor's love, by listening for her beautiful <u>koto</u> playing. In the score of the Sakamoto edition of this piece,
an inscription after measure 249 makes this plea: "The
tomb of Kogo no Tsubone is in Arashiyama, Kyoto, near the
bridge of Togetsukyo. If you go there, please burn
incense in front of her tomb."

---

[2] Other examples of "improved songs" are Kikutomi
Kengyō's "Minatogawa" with the "Sāmushiro" <u>tegoto</u>,
Kikuyama Kengyō's "Chiyu no Tomo" with the "Chāondo"
<u>tegoto</u>, Kikunaka Kengyō's "Matsu no Homare" with the
"Noyama no Goko" <u>tegoto</u> (Fujita, Tonan 1932: 459).

"Aki no Koto no Ha." Sources agree that "Aki no
Koto no Ha" was composed by a shamisen player, Nishiyama
Tokumoto. According to Fujita (1934: 79) Nishiyama went
to Osaka at the beginning of the Meiji era to study honte
kumiuta shamisen, but studied koto there, as well. Fujita
asserts that Nishiyama "studied koto one-half year and
composed 'Aki no Koto no Ha,'" following the form of the
kokingumi. If indeed he wrote the piece while in Osaka
early in Meiji it must have been patterned after "Chidori"
because "Aki no Koto no Ha" is a tegotomono and only
"Chidori" of the Kokingumi had a tegoto at that time.
Although "Aki no Koto no Ha" is performed by musicians in
the Yamada school, it has not been published in Yamada
score.

"Shin Takasago." The published Ikuta score (Miyagi
edition) which customarily gives the composer's name
attributes "Shin Takasago" to "anonymous"; the Yamada
score gives Terashima Hanano of late nineteenth century
as the composer. Fujita Tonan (1932: 461 and 1934: 110)
agrees, places him in mid-Meiji period and adds that he
was from Nagoya. In the Meikyoku Kaidai Fujita states
that Terashima "composed the koto music . . . for the
shamisen piece 'Takasago,' thus it is called 'Shin (New)
Takasago.'" (1934: 110) It appears then that "Shin
Takasago" is an arrangement of a shamisen tegotomono and
should provide yet another dimension for stylistic
comparison.

The tunings (chōshi) in which these five compositions were written are also related to the historical
developments in koto music through the nineteenth century.
Some tunings and the manner in which they were used were
continuation of earlier tradition and others were

innovation. In koto kumiuta there was a long-standing
practice of changing the chōshi in the middle of a
composition. It was done in late seventeenth-century
compositions and was common in the first half of the
eighteenth century, mainly in kumiuta by Mitsuhashi
Kengyō (d. 1760) (Adriaansz 1973: 38). This practice
continued in tegotomono and other types of shamisen
music as well as in koto tegotomono.

   Ensemble performance of the instruments opened the
way to new musical possibilities. In the Tempō Period
(1830-1843) when efforts were being made to equalize
the parts in the koto-shamisen ensemble and also to
extricate the koto from the hegemony of the shamisen,
Ichiura Kengyō of Osaka was among the first to experiment.
He tried arranging honte-kaede shamisen pieces to shamisen honte-koto kaede and put the shamisen on a tuning
higher or lower than that of the koto (Fujita, Tonan
1932: 455). He also arranged honte-kaede shamisen pieces
for honte-kaede koto, assigning high and low tunings to
the two kotos. For instance, he combined hirajōshi with
oranda jōshi, a tuning devised from the Western major
scale and named for the Hollanders who introduced it.
The high-low idea was eventually utilized by many composers, as was the derivation of new tunings. The high
tuning for "Mikuni no Homare," a patriotic composition
of early Meiji, for example, was supposedly the pentatonic
scale taken from Chinese popular music (called kankan
chōshi) and the low from Western music (Fujita, Tonan
1932: 459). In the next section of this chapter, the
subject of chōshi will be discussed further.

Tunings

The thirteen strings of the koto are tuned by
positioning moveable wood, ivory, or plastic bridges (ji)
at the proper places along the length of the instrument.
Even in notation the strings are referred to by number
rather than by pitch; string 1 is the farthest from the
player. For solo koto performance the pitch for string 1
is generally accepted to be "d above middle c" on the
piano.[3] In duo-koto performances if the two kotos are
to be tuned differently the score will indicate a pair
of strings in the honte and kaede which are tuned to the
same pitch and the remainder can be derived from that.

When played in sankyoku ensemble the pitch for koto
string 1 is taken from the shakuhachi which is the only
instrument of the ensemble (koto, shamisen, shakuhachi)
with fixed pitches. In the dictionary of koto tunings,
Gendai Sōkyoku Chōshi Jiten, a shakuhachi pitch is given
with the name of the chōshi for each composition listed,
including many that are not performed in sankyoku
ensemble.[4] In many cases the listing specifies to which
school of shakuhachi playing the pitch designation
belongs, for the names of the pitches vary among them.
For example, the shakuhachi pitch names for the two
leading schools, Kinko ryū and Tozan (Tsuyama) ryū, are
below in Chart 3 (Malm 1959: 271). In the Chōshi Jiten

---

[3] Notated in Charts 4 and 5 below as pitch "e" in
order to avoid the necessity for numerous accidentals.
The transcriptions of the compositions do not all conform with the pitch registers in these charts.

[4] Chōshi becomes jōshi in a compound such as
hirajoshi ("hira" plus "chōshi").

Chart 3:   <u>Shakuhachi</u> Pitch Names

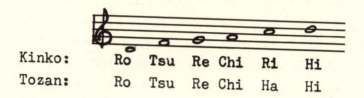

Kinko:	Ro	Tsu	Re	Chi	Ri	Hi
Tozan:	Ro	Tsu	Re	Chi	Ha	Hi

it is stated that for the composition "Chidori" in
<u>kokinjōshi</u> (tuning) string 1 should be set to <u>shakuhachi</u>
pitch Ro; for "Aki no Koto no Ha" in <u>hirajōshi</u> it should
be set to <u>shakuhachi</u> Kinko <u>ryū</u> pitch Ri, Tsuyama <u>ryū</u> pitch
Ha. For some compositions more than one suitable start-
ing pitch is suggested in the dictionary; for compositions
in <u>nakazorajōshi</u>, for instance, string 1 could be pitched
to <u>shakuhachi</u> Ro, Re, or Chi. <u>Shakuhachi</u> pitches are
specified on published scores of many <u>koto</u> compositions,
as well.

These <u>koto</u> tunings have five basic pitches; those
five forming the characteristic "octave" are bracketed
in the charts below which give the tunings used in
"Chidori," "Haru no Kyoku," "Saga no Aki," "Aki no Koto
no Ha," and "Shin Takasago." Those five pitches are
duplicated or doubled at the octave(s) on the remaining
strings: strings 1 and 5 (or in rare cases 1 and 4) are
tuned to the same pitch; 2, 7, and 12 are three octaves
of the same pitch and likewise 3, 8, and 13; 4 and 9,
6 and 11 are octaves. Exceptions to this do occur, and
they will be pointed out where pertinent.

In each tuning at least two pitches are more
important than the others; those two are usually at the
interval of a fifth from each other. In the tuning
charts below, the base pitch is indicated by a large

arrow and the fifth by a smaller arrow. The pitch
hierarchy of a tuning is particularly emphasized and
exploited in the song sections of tegotomono.

Eight different tunings are used in these compositions: 1) hirajōshi, 2) nakazorajōshi, 3) Takasago-
kumoijōshi, 4) kokinjōshi, and 5) four tunings not given
names. The named tunings are shown in Chart 4 and are
discussed in that order.

Chart 4:   Named Tunings in the Compositions

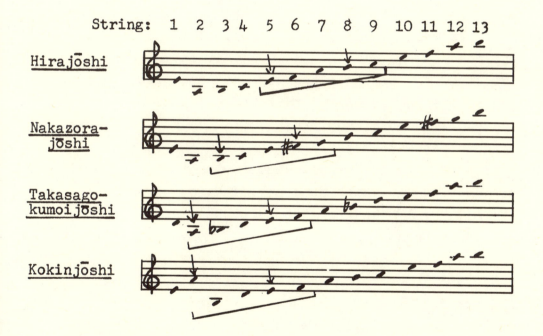

Hirajōshi. Until the Edo period the primary tuning
used for koto compositions by Tsukushi-goto musicians
was derived from the gagaku scales (Adriaansz 1973: 33).
The gagaku seven-tone scales had five basic pitches and
two auxiliary ones; in ritsu mode the auxiliary tones

were the third and seventh degrees of the scale. In
Chart 5(a) below ritsu mode is given with the auxiliary
pitches in black notes; they were not employed as
pitches in the Tsukushi-goto tuning which consequently
had no semitones (Chart 5b). In the first half of the
seventeenth century Yatsuhashi Kengyō, the blind musician who popularized koto music away from its elitist
sphere, introduced a new tuning, hirajōshi, which was
related to a scale used in popular shamisen music, the
In scale (Chart 5c).[5]

According to Adriaansz the In scale, too, had five
basic tones; pitches sho and u̅ each had a raised (ei)
form, as well (1973: 33). The raised forms were used
in ascending melody and the original forms in descent,
but since the ei-sho pitch was not used frequently,
there were two ascending patterns. The ascent and
descent without ei-sho are given in Chart 5(d). The
descent pattern appears in hirajōshi (Chart 5e).[6]
Hirajōshi is a frequently used tuning to the present
day and the one which students of koto learn first
(Malm 1959: 178 and Piggott 1909: 46-47).

Nakazorajōshi. "Aki no Koto no Ha" begins in
hirajōshi, but halfway through the tegoto the tuning of
both kotos must be changed to nakazorajōshi for the
remainder of the piece: strings 6 and 11 are raised a
semitone, 7 and 12 lowered a tone. (The pitches in

[5] Sources for Chart 5 are: (a) Malm (1959) 101;
(b) Adriaansz (1973) 34; (c) Adriaansz (1973) 33 and
Malm (1959) 160; (d) Adriaansz (1973) 33.

[6] The descent pattern is the form of the In scale
given in Kitahara (1966) 275.

Chart 5: Derivation of Hirajōshi

Charts 6-10 correspond to those in the complete trans-
scriptions.) This is accomplished without interrupting
the flow of the melody, for it is done with the left
hand as the right hand continues playing. The composer
allowed time for the strings to be retuned in this
manner: string 12 is last struck in m. 177, string 6
in m. 181, string 11 in m. 185, and string 7 in m. 186;
the changes can therefore be made gradually between
ms. 177 and 190. A slight ritard to mark the end of

Chart 6:   "Aki no Koto no Ha" Tunings

dan I provides additional time.

The melodic base of the tuning is thus shifted
a fifth higher than that of hirajōshi, but the interval
structure of the characteristic octaves of the two
tunings is the same: semitone, major third, tone,
semitone.   Nakazorajōshi was added to the repertoire of
koto tunings by Ikuta Kengyō in the eighteenth century
and was used in this same manner in kumiuta composed in
the first half of that century, for instance in "Haru no
Miya" by Mitsuhashi Kengyō (d. 1760) in which the tuning
changed from hirajōshi to nakazorajōshi to okebonejōshi
a fifth from nakazorajōshi (Adriaansz 1973: 38).

Takasago-kumoijōshi.   Kumoijōshi (from which
Takasago-kumoijōshi was derived) and hirajōshi were both
products of the seventeenth century.   The interval
structure of their characteristic octaves is the same,
but in kumoi the pitch of string 13 is a semitone higher.
(See Chart 7.)   The base pitch of kumoijōshi is a fourth
higher than that of hirajōshi.   Some of the earliest
instances of change of chōshi mid-kumiuta were from
hirajōshi to kumoijōshi: "Wakaba" by Kitajima Kengyō
(d. 1690) and "Makino" (Adriaansz 1973: 38, 455).

Chart 7: Derivation of Takasago-kumoijōshi

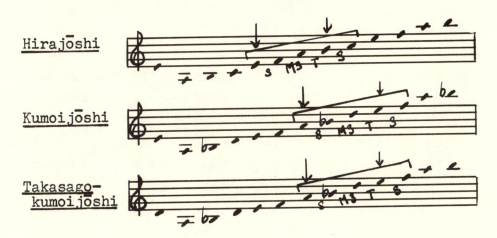

Hirajōshi

Kumoijōshi

Takasago-
kumoijōshi

For Takasago-kumoijōshi the pitch of string 1 is
lowered a whole step so that the fifth from base pitch
is less emphasized and the interval of a fourth more
emphasized; the structure of the characteristic octave
is left intact. No change of tuning occurs in "Shin
Takasago," but the honte and kaede parts are in different tunings: Takasago-kumoijōshi for Koto I is paired
with hirajōshi in a lower register for Koto II. They
fit together well because they are the same mode at
different pitch levels, extending the range a fifth
lower.

Chart 8: "Shin Takasago" Tunings

Takasago-
kumoijōshi

Hirajōshi

Kokinjōshi. Kokinjōshi was devised by Yoshizawa
Kengyō as the tuning for "Chidori," for "Haru no Kyoku"
and the three other kokingumi. In the Miyagi edition
of the Ikuta ryū "Chidori" score, the instructions for
tuning a koto to kokinjōshi are changes to be made from
hirajōshi as demonstrated in Chart 9: first raise the
fourth string one step and "make harmony" with the
second string; next raise the ninth string one step as
was done with the fourth; finally, raise the second
string to produce the same pitch as that of string
seven (33rd printing, 1964). The interval structure of
the characteristic octave of kokinjōshi is different
from any discussed above: descending minor seventh,
ascending minor third, tone, semitone. The change of
tuning did not disturb that octave.

Chart 9: Derivation of "Haru no Kyoku" Tunings

Hirajōshi

Haru no Kyoku:
Kokinjōshi

Unnamed tuning

When the string 2 pitch is raised an octave higher
than usual the tuning assumes the shape of a tuning for
gaku-sō, the koto in the gagaku ensemble. In gaku-sō

chōshi an ascending fourth is followed by a descending seventh (Adriaansz 1973: 17 and Kishibe 1969: 21)[7] Yoshizawa not only used tenth-century court texts for the kokingumi, but also utilized the shape of a court orchestra gaku-sō tuning.

"Chidori" remains in kokinjōshi from beginning to end. The kaede tegoto added by Matsuzaka Harue is also in kokinjōshi and at the same pitch register.

The tegoto which Matsuzaka Harue added to "Haru no Kyoku" begins in kokinjōshi for a smooth transition from the mae-uta (supposedly with a Yoshizawa ai-no-te), but after seven measures the tuning is to be changed to one not given a name. The pitch of string 8 is lowered a half-step to create a pitch not duplicated elsewhere in the chōshi, and the thirteenth string pitch is raised a step and a half to form an octave with string 9 (see Chart 9). Lowering pitch 8 increases the possibility of tension in the melodic line, because a tritone is present between it and the second strongest pitch in the tuning. In addition, the descending leading tone to the base pitch leans more strongly in that direction from only a half-step above. By raising the pitch of string 13, the melodic range is extended. With the pitch of string 3 (usually the lowest octave of strings

---

[7] Harich-Schneider (1973) 123 gives the gaku-sō tuning in banjiki-chō as it is done now; the pitch of string 2 is apparently no longer raised, so the shape of the chōshi is the same as in sōkyoku tunings. Adriaansz states further that kokinjōshi is related to gaku-sō banshiki-chō; strings 6 and 11 are a whole step higher in the latter.

3, 8, and 13) left as it was, the possibility of melodic
variety at different pitch registers in inherent.

At the beginning of the second dan of the tegoto,
the tuning is reset to kokinjoshi to lead back into the
ato-uta. The tuning scheme of "Haru no Kyoku" is:

Mae-uta	Tegoto		Ato-uta
	Dan I	Dan II	
Kokinjoshi	Unnamed choshi	Kokinjoshi	Kokinjoshi
(Yoshizawa)	(Matsuzaka)	(Matsuzaka)	(Yoshizawa).

Unnamed choshi. The tunings for the two kotos in
"Saga no Aki" are not given names either in the Choshi
Jiten or in the published scores. As shown in Chart 10
they include no semitones. Although tunings for the
gaku-so and also the Tsukushi-goto tuning were without
semitones, sources do not attribute this to another
attempt to utilize former koto tradition. Rather, it
is more likely to be an example of a newly-derived
tuning.

Chart 10: "Saga no Aki" Tunings

Koto I in "Saga no Aki" is pitched a fifth higher
than Koto II, but they share the same characteristic
octave and pitch hierarchy. The interval structure on
strings 1, 2, and 3 of Koto I differs from that on

strings 1 and 2 of Koto II in order to extend the range
without disturbing the "mode"; it is only important that
the interval structure of the two characteristic octaves
be the same. This is an example of the high-low tuning
with which a number of compositions were written around
the beginning of the Meiji period and is the same
principle as combining Takasago-kumoijōshi with hirajōshi in "Shin Takasago."

Tuning pitches are not the only pitches available.
Additional pitches a half step, whole step, even one and
one-half steps above open string pitch are produced by
the oshide technique (see page 26 above). Both primary
(especially in "Saga no Aki") and non-primary (especially
in "Shin Takasago") tuning pitches are pressed for oshide.
Through the five compositions oshide fall most often on
the strong halves of beats and frequently on the first
and third beats in measures; in "Aki no Koto no Ha" they
occur on the first and fourth beats predominantly.
Charts 11 and 12 show all pitches used in the koto parts
of each composition, both in the tuning and created by
oshide.

Characteristic Melodic Material

A few melodic elements appear to be particularly
characteristic of writing for the koto. Lower and upper
neighbor tones are rampant. Motivic repetitions with
variations or in transposition and sequences of a sort
idiomatic to this music are scattered throughout.
Descending melodic motives, too, appear to be prominent.

The lower neighbor tone is present in one of the
only melodic motives which recur consistently in all

Chart 11: Pitches in the <u>Honte</u>

- Pitches in tuning
- Tuning pitches also created by <u>oshide</u>
- Pitches created by <u>oshide</u>

Chidori <u>Kokinjōshi</u>

Haru no Kyoku <u>Kokinjōshi</u>

Haru no Kyoku Unnamed <u>Chōshi</u>

Saga no Aki Unnamed <u>chōshi</u>

Shin Takasago <u>Takasago-kumoijōshi</u>

Aki no Koto no Ha <u>Hirajōshi</u>

Aki no Koto no Ha <u>Nakazorajōshi</u>

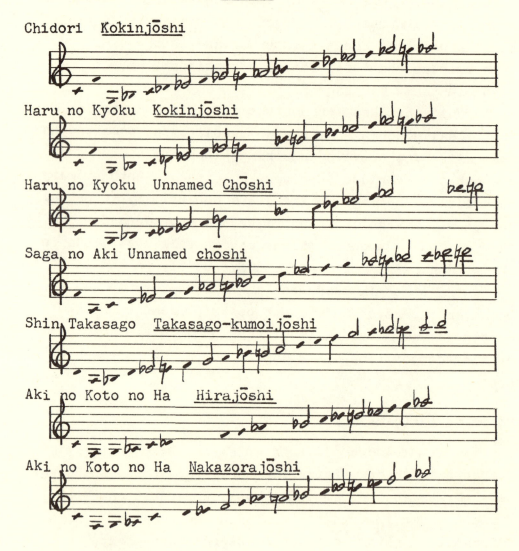

these pieces. Example 1(a) gives the skeleton version
of the motive; it can be found inverted and in various
forms. In Example 1(b) the lower neighbor tone is used

Chart 12: Pitches in the <u>Kaede</u>

- Pitches in tuning
- Tuning pitches also created by <u>oshide</u>
- Pitches created by <u>oshide</u>

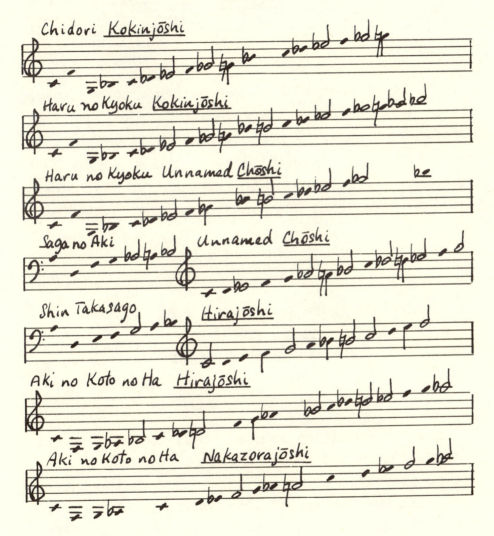

to extend that motive within a longer phrase. See also ms. 77-78 in the transcription of "Aki no Koto no Ha" where the motive is used as a connecting device between two phrases.

Example 1

(a)   (b) Aki no Koto no Ha

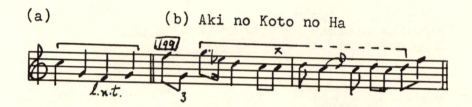

In some instances the lower neighbor tone pattern is better described as a lower string tone pattern. The melody falls on adjacent <u>koto</u> strings as is usual, but as in Example 2 the interval between those strings is wider than a whole step due to the tuning. Most often, however, the two tones are a major or minor second apart.

Example 2

Saga no Aki
String: 4 5 4 5   6   7 6 6 6   7

Motivic repetition and transposition such as that shown in Example 3 are also common. Repetition of a melodic motive three or more times in succession (termed a sequence in Western music) also occurs in these compositions. A sequence peculiarly characteristic of this <u>koto</u> music is quoted in Example 4. Intervallic differences are due to the tuning, for this is played entirely on adjacent open strings.

Example 3

Saga no Aki

Example 4

Chidori
String:

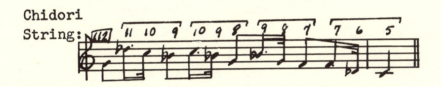

Summary

The composition of these five tegotomono spans
much of the nineteenth century; they are listed below
in tentative chronological order. "Haru no Kyoku" is
listed by when it became a tegotomono.

"Chidori" Around mid-nineteenth century
        (Between Tempo Period [1930-1843]
        and beginning of Meiji [1868])

"Saga no Aki" Mid-nineteenth century

"Aki no Koto no Ha" Mid- to late nineteenth
        century

"Shin Takasago" Late nineteenth century

"Haru no Kyoku" End nineteenth century

They span the development of nineteenth-century sōkyoku
from an arrangement for koto of a shamisen piece, to an
early solo koto tegotomono with kaede juxtaposed, to duo-
koto tegotomono in non-traditional and traditional tunings.

It appears that the tuning provides the basic melodic material for a composition, because melodic lines
tend largely to follow the pitches of adjacent open
strings.   Octave patterns such as warizume, kakezume, and
hayakake create temporary diversions from and prolongation
of the motives that fall on successive strings.

A change of chōshi in the course of a piece had been
common practice in kumiuta composition since mid-eighteenth
century but writing for two kotos in different tunings was
a nineteenth-century development, one associated particularly with tegoto and therefore with tegotomono.   The
tunings used in these five compositions are summarized in
Chart 13; the tuning is relisted in a different section
only if a change occurs.

Chart 13:   Tunings Schemes of the Five Compositions

```
——————— No kaede
. . . . . Continues
```

		Mae-uta	Tegoto	Ato-uta
Chidori	I:	Kokinjōshi · · · · · · · · · · · · · · · · ·
	II:	———————	Kokinjōshi	—————
Haru no	I:	Kokinjōshi	Kokin——Unnamed——Kokin	Kokin
Kyoku	II:	———————	————— Same Same	Same
Aki no	I:	Hirajōshi	Hirajōshi——Nakazora	Nakazora
Koto no	II:	———————	Same Same	—————
Ha				
Saga no	I:	Unnamed · · · · · · · · · · · · · · · · ·
Aki	II:	Unnamed · · · · · · · · · · · · · · · · ·
		(Fifth lower)		
Shin	I:	Takasago-kumoijōshi · · · · · · · · · · · · · · · ·
Takasago	II:	Hirajōshi · · · · · · · · · · · · · · · ·
		(Fifth lower)		

FOUR / *Uta,* Part I: The Song

Poetic Texts

     The texts for four of these five <u>tegotomono</u> were
taken from major literary sources. From the great
poetry collections, the <u>Kokinshū</u> and <u>Kinyoshū</u>, came the
uta for "Chidori no Kyoku" and "Haru no Kyoku." The
"Shin Takasago" text was derived from the Nō drama,
<u>Takasago</u>, and that of "Saga no Aki" from the epic <u>Heike</u>
<u>Monogatari</u>. The text of "Aki no Koto no Ha" was newly
written for the <u>koto</u> piece by an anonymous poet.

     The <u>Kokinshū</u>, completed about the year 905 A.D.,
was the first of twenty-one imperial anthologies to be
ordered by a succession of emperors between the eighth
and the tenth centuries. Its title defines its contents--
<u>Collection</u> <u>of</u> <u>Ancient</u> <u>and</u> <u>Modern</u> <u>Times</u>, the modern times
being the Heian period (894-1185) when the capital had
been moved from Nara to Kyoto. At the Heian courts
poetry was so much a part of daily life that it was a
spontaneous means of communication.

     The poems selected for the twenty volumes of the
<u>Kokinshū</u> range from a series on each of the seasons, to
congratulatory verse, to thoughts on parting, travel,
love, and names of things. The text of the <u>mae-uta</u> of

"Chidori" is from the seventh section, "Ga no Uta" ("Poems of Congratulations") that were usually addressed to members of the imperial family or other members of the aristocracy on such occasions as birthdays. "Shio no yama" is addressed to the Emperor, but the particular occasion for its composition is not known (Brower and Miner 1961: 194). Chidori are sea plovers, birds that fly between Honshu and Shikoku islands and live on the beaches.

"Chidori" mae-uta

Shio no yama
Sashide no iso ni
Sumuchidori
Kimi ga miyo oba
Yachio tozo naku.

Kimi ga miyo oba
Yachio tozo naku.
    (Kokinshū, No. 345)

Plovers themselves that
    nestle on Mount Shio
And Sashide-on-Sea, as thou
    must know--
They sing a wish thy reign
Thousands of years may attain.
    (Wakameda 1922: 83)

     The text of "Awajishima," the ato-uta of "Chidori", was taken from the fifth imperial anthology, the Kinyoshū (Collection of Golden Leaves), compiled by Minamoto Shunrai between 1124 and 1127. The collection of 416 poems on ten scrolls was considered radical in its day since it included verses by contemporary poets whose writing was less elegant than that of their predecessors (Brower and Miner 1961: 241). The Suma Gate mentioned in the poem was one of the many gates throughout the countryside where the luggage of travelers was inspected.

"Chidori" ato-uta

Awajishima
Kayou chidori no
Naku koe ni
Ikuyo nezamenu
Suma no seki mori.

Guardian of the gate of
Suma, how many nights have
you awakened at the crying
of the shore bird of the
Isle of Awaji?
    (Keene 1955: 95)

Ikuyo nezamenu
Suma no seki mori.
  (Kinyoshū, Scroll 4)

The six verses in "Haru no Kyoku" are all from
the first two scrolls of the Kokinshū, "Songs of Spring."
Though selected from throughout the two scrolls, they
appear in the koto piece in the order in which they
appear in the collection. The translations below are
from Wakameda (1922: 5, 6, 13, 27, 28, 30).

"Haru no Kyoku" mae-uta

A. Uguisu no   But for an uguisu's sweet
    Tani yori izuru   cry
    Koe nakuba   That comes out of the vale,
    Haru kuru koto o   Who knows but spring steals
    Tareka shiramashi.   from the sky
        (Kokinshū, No. 14)   Down and over the vale.
        Ōye no Chisato

B. Miyama ni wa   In the deep mountains e'en
    Matsu no yuki dani   the snow
    Kienakuni   Upon the pines remains
    Miyako wa nobe no   But we pluck in the Miyako
    Wakana tsumikeri.   Young grass in fields and
        (Kokinshū, No. 19)   plains.
        Anonymous, purpose
        unknown

C. Yo no naka ni   If there were in the world
    Taete sakura no   no cherry trees
    Nakariseba   The heart in spring would
    Haru no kokoro wa   be set more at ease.[1]
    Nodokekaramashita.
        (Kokinshū, No. 53)
        Ariwara no Narihira
        Lines composed on seeing
        the cherry blossoms at
        the Nagisa-no-In.

[1] Compare this translation with that on p. 59.

D. Koma nabete   Let us proceed on horse-
    Izami ni yukan   back now:
    Furusato wa   In our old town
    Yuki to komikoso   The cherry blossoms just
    Hana ya chirurame.   like snow,
        (Kokinshū, No. 111)   They will fall down.
        Anonymous, purpose
        unknown.

"Haru no Kyoku" ato-uta

A. Wagayado ni   Wisterias have bloomed at
    Sakeru fujinami   my dwelling place;
    Tachikaeri   E'en passers-by may stop
    Sugigate ni nomi   and see their grace.
    Hito no mirurame.
        (Kokinshū, No. 120)
        Oshikochi no Mitsume
        Lines composed on seeing
        some passers-by stop and
        view the wisterias at my
        bower.

B. Koe taezu   Without repose, I say,
    Nakeyo uguisu   Pour thy melodious notes
    Hitotose ni   I hear
    Futatabi to dani   O uguisu, I pray––
    Kubeki haru kawa.   The spring will not come
        (Kokinshū, No. 131)   twice a year.
        Okikaze
        Lines composed at a poetical
        meeting held by the Empress
        in the times of Kampyo.

The poetry in the imperial anthologies was waka,
or court poetry in Japanese style rather than in the
popular Chinese style. The verses in "Chidori" and "Haru
no Kyoku" are the particular type of waka called tanka.
Each verse in tanka poetic form consists of five lines
in the syllabic grouping 5-7-5-7-7. In the last verse
given above, for instance, the syllables were divided:

Ko-e ta-e-zu (5)

Na-ke-yo u-gu-i-su (7)

Hi-to-to-se ni (5)

Fu-ta-ta-bi to da-ni (7)

Ku-be-ki ha-ru ka-wa. (7)

By the time the <u>Kokinshū</u> was compiled the regularization
of the number of syllables in a line to 5 or 7 had already
been a practice for at least two hundred years and even
the <u>tanka</u> form was traditional (Brower and Miner 1961: 86).

In the period when the <u>Kokinshū</u> <u>tanka</u> were written
the syntax of the verses usually called for a pause after
the first and third lines, resulting in a gradual lengthening of phrases from 5 syllables, to 12 (7 plus 5), to
14 (7 plus 7) syllables. The sense of the verse carried
through the pauses to the last word to complete the idea
of the poem. Each line hinged on the next, or described
the next, so that the whole would be an integral unit
inseparable into independent lines.

The syntax of <u>tanka</u> form was carried out to some
extent when the texts were set to melody. In the chart
below the syntax is written: 5 ➥ 12 ➥ 14; under each of
those units is shown the number of "measures" (groupings
of four beats as in Ikuta scores) of melody to which
those syllables have been set. In the "Chidori" <u>mae-uta</u>,
for example, the melody to "Shio no yama" (5 syllables)
takes four measures; after a pause of one measure the
second cluster of 12 syllables "Sashide no iso ni Sumu
chidori" takes eleven measures, and so forth.[2] The

_____

[2] See the transcriptions. If two beats of a four
beat measure were filled, it was counted as a full

measure units become progressively longer as the syllable
units do, but the pause between the 5 syllable phrase and
12 syllable phrase was not consistently maintained.

Chart 14:   Tanka Syntax and Melodic Setting
Length of Units

Tanka	(Syll.)	5	♩	12	♩	14	♩	‖: 14
Chidori								
Mae-uta	(Ms.)	4	1	11	6	12	11	‖: 12
Ato-uta		3	0	6	6	11	5	‖: 11
Haru no Kyoku								
Mae-uta A		4	1	7	0	9	4	
B		4	0	8	1	12	3	
C		5	0	10	3	11	4	
D		3	0	6	1	7		
Ato-uta A		4	0	8	1	9	4	
B		4½	0	8½	0	9		

Stated another way, it can be seen that the syntax
of the poetic lines was kept only in the mae-uta of
"Chidori." The following chart shows the lines as they
were grouped in musical units when set to melody.

An examination of the third poem in "Haru no Kyoku"
will explain more thoroughly the complexity of a tanka
and a reason why the tanka of this period are considered

---

measure; if less than two beats, not as a full measure.
It becomes difficult to give precise lengths for ai-no-
te in the "Haru" ato-uta because honte and kaede overlap
with each other and with the song phrases.

Chart 15:   <u>Tanka</u> Syntax and Melodic Setting
Grouping of Lines

<u>Tanka</u>	Lines Grouped in Setting			
Chidori				
<u>Mae-uta</u>	1	2 & 3	4 & 5	4 & 5
<u>Ato-uta</u>	1 - 3		4 & 5	4 & 5
Haru no Kyoku				
<u>Mae-uta</u> A	1	2 - 5		
B	1 - 3		4 & 5	
C	1 - 3		4 & 5	
D	1 - 3		4 & 5	
<u>Ato-uta</u> A	1 - 3		4 & 5	
B	1 - 5			

masterpieces in Japanese literature.

5	Yo no naka ni	If cherry flowers
12	Taete sakura no Nakariseba	Had never come into this world, The hearts of men
14	Naru no kokoro wa Nodokekaramashi.	Would have kept their tranquil freedom Even at the brilliant height of spring. (Brower and Miner 1961: 199)

"The major pause at the end of the third line anticipates
the strong conclusion, in which the 'o' and 'k' sounds of
the preceding line are given a new direction; the first
and fourth lines have slightly longer pauses and their
grammatical structure is similar, except that each of the
two nouns in the fourth line [<u>naru</u>, <u>kokoro</u>] has one more
syllable than the corresponding noun [<u>yo</u>, <u>naka</u>] in the

first line." (Brower and Miner 1961: 199)

 To each of the "Chidori" <u>tanka</u> was added a repetition of the last two lines. The text repetition in the "Chidori" <u>mae-uta</u> was reinforced by a repeat of the melody, as well. In the <u>ato-uta</u>, however, the repetition was set to a different melody.

 The text of "Saga no Aki" is based on an incident in the thirteenth-century <u>Heike</u> <u>Monogatari</u> (<u>Tale</u> <u>of</u> <u>the</u> <u>Heike</u>) attributed to Yukinaga Nakayama (1159?-ca. 1221). This great epic narrative relates the struggle for power between the great ruling clan of the twelfth century, the Heike, and their rival, the Genji clan, and the eventual tragic end of the Heike family. It has transmitted through the centuries the teachings of <u>bushido</u>, the warrior's code of ethics and the weltanschauung of the medieval Japanese. Its heroes and heroines were those of the children for succeeding centuries, and even now remain alive in the imagination of the Japanese people. The <u>Heike</u> <u>Monogatari</u> survives as a document of historic importance and as a great literary achievement of its time. Episodes from this long poem were recited melodically in every corner of the islands by itinerant singers accompanying themselves on a <u>biwa</u>. It provided the tales for <u>kōwaka</u>, the ballad drama performed by <u>samurai</u> in the sixteenth century, for popular fables, for the Nō drama, <u>kabuki</u>, and puppet plays.

 The text of the <u>koto</u> piece "Saga no Aki" is related to the episode in which a trusted warrior, Nakakune, has been sent by the Emperor to search for a young female attendant of the Imperial Palace, Kogo no Tsubone, who had left the court. Since here whereabouts are unknown, he is to listen for her exceptionally beautiful <u>koto</u>

koto playing, and recognize her by it. In the Sakamoto
edition of the koto score the uta is explained: "[The
setting is an] autumn evening in Saga. Saga is known as
a place of loneliness, especially on such an evening.
The moon is shining and I can hear the sound of a koto
which comes from the door of a humble home and I wonder
if that music might be the storm blowing on the peaks
of mountains or the wind blowing through pine trees or
the music played by the person for whom I am looking.
I stop my horse and I realize that sound is a song of
love, of someone yearning for her beloved."

"Saga no Aki"   "Autumn at Saga"

Mae-uta

Saradedani   Even if it had not been so,
Mono no samishiki   The area around Saga would be
Na ni tateru   known for its loneliness.
                              On autumn evenings when the
Saga no atari no   moon is brilliant,
Aki no koro   The sound of the koto steal-
Tsuki wa kumanaki   ing out from the brushwood
Shiba no to ni   door---

Shinobite morase
Koto no ne wa

Mine no arashi ka   Is it a storm in the mountain
Matsukaze ka   crags?
Tazunuru hito no   Or the wind rustling through
Susabi kaya   the pines?
                              Perhaps it is entertainment
                                  for some visitor.

Ato-uta

Koma o todomete   Stopping my horse to listen,
Kiku toki wa   I hear clearly the sound of
Tsumaoto shiruki   fingers plucking Soofuren
Soofuren

Tsumaoto shiruki   Clearly the sound of fingers
Soofuren.   plucking Soofuren.
                                   (Shawn O'Malley, UCLA
                                  1967)

The <u>samurai</u> succeeds in finding her, as we are told
in the <u>Heike</u> <u>Monogatari</u> but not in this song, and the
girl blesses the Emperor with a child. Soon after she
is spirited off to a nunnery by enemies of the Emperor,
who dies shortly thereafter. It is not important that
the full story is left unfinished in the <u>koto</u> <u>uta</u>, for
the tale is common knowledge to those who will hear it.

The poem of "Saga no Aki" is not in <u>tanka</u> form, but
its lines are alternately of 5 and 7 syllables. <u>Koto</u>
interludes occur in the <u>uta</u> at those points where a line
is skipped in the text given above. The subdivisions
correspond with the shifts in the poem, so that the
irregular musical form is determined by the sensitive
setting of the text. Although the poem is divided into

<u>Mae-uta</u>
  Number of poetry lines
  grouped in a unit: 3 ⌐ 4 ⌐ 2 ⌐ 4
  Number of measures: 9 3 13 1 5 12 12

<u>Ato-uta</u>
        Poetry lines: 4 ⌐ ‖: 2
          Measures: 14 5   7

<u>mae-uta</u> and <u>ato-uta</u>, the episode it relates ends only
at the end of the <u>ato-uta</u>. The final two lines of text
are repeated but the melody to which they are set changes.

The text of "Shin Takasago" was taken from the Nō
drama <u>Takasago</u> by Zeami Motokiyo (1363-1443). The play
in turn was based on a legend mentioned in the prose
Preface to the <u>Kokinshū</u> in which a pine tree in Takasago
and a pine tree in Sumiyoshi are believed to be twin
pines, man and wife, and symbols of longevity and
conjugal fidelity. The spirit of the Sumiyoshi pine
crossed to Takasago each night for countless years to

visit his wife who lived on the coast of the Bay of Takasago.   They had become white-haired, but the bond which
united them defied time and age.   At the beginning of the
play, a Shinto priest and his attendants are on their way
by sea from Kyushu and land at Takasago to visit its
famous pine tree.   It is a spring evening, and an aged
couple are raking up the fallen needles under the tree.
The priest asks and is told of the twin pine.   He decides
to visit Sumiyoshi, asks how to get there, and sets out
on the journey depicted in this song.   In the drama this
song is the machi-utai ("waiting song") chanted by the
second main actor (waki) and his attendants as a transition to the denouement of the play when the main actor
(shite) reappears on stage.   The melody of the machi-
utai was not retained in the koto composition.

"Shin Takasago"

Mae-uta

Takasago ya	From Takasago Bay,
Kono urabune ni	Hoisting our sails,
Ho o agete	Under the climbing moon
Tsuki morotomoni	We put out on the flowing
Ideshio no	tide.
Nami no Awaji no	Leaving behind the isle
Shimakage ya	of Awaji[3]

Ato-uta

Tooku Naruo no	And passing distant Naruo
Oki sugite	To Suminoye we have come,
Haya Suminoe ni	
Tsukinikeri.	
Haya Suminoe ni	To Suminoye we have come.
Tsukinikeri.	(The Noh Drama 1955: 14)

[3] An island separating the Bay of Osaka from the
western part of the Inland Sea.

The poetic form of "Shin Takasago," too, is an alternation of lines of 5 and 7 syllables. Whereas the original Nō text is eleven lines without a break, the koto uta version is thirteen lines divided into seven in the mae-uta and six in the ato-uta. While the Nō song has only the last line repeated, the last two lines of the ato-uta of "Shin Takasago" are repeated. Text repetition is supported by melodic repetition.

"Aki no Koto no Ha" has a newly-composed text, but on a traditional subject--a season. Among the four seasons of the year, autumn is the most frequently used as a topic for poetry. In contrast to the composed feeling of spring, the poetry of autumn is mostly meloncholy. This song depicts that mood by using words such as "dew," "insects," "kinuta" (the pounding of clothes to clean them), and "moon." When the leaves of the pawlonia (kiri) tree fall, it is a sign that autumn is coming; the insects which have beautiful voices weep in the garden because they suffer from frost. The heart of the poet moves with the sound of the kinuta in the night when the full moon is in the height of the sky.

"Aki no Koto no Ha"　　　　　　　　　"Autumn Words"

Mae-uta

Chiri somuru	By the leaves of the paw-
Kiri no hite ha ni	lownia beginning to fall,
Onozukara	And being cool in my long-
Temoto suzushiku	sleeved robe,
Asa yuu wa.	I have come to know the
	sadness of the dew
	Falling morning and night
	on the grasses of the moor.
Nobe no chigusa ni	Who, pausing at the sound
Oku tsuyu no	of the pine crickets,
Tsuyu no nasake o	Was attracted by still more
Mi ni shiru ya	lovely

Tare matsumushi no
Ni ni tatete.
Itodo yasashiki
Suzumushi no
Koe ni hikarete
Mononofu no
Ayumasu koma no
Kutsuwamushi.

Calls of "bell ring" insects
And then was distracted by
    the noise of the saddle bugs
    of a warrior's horse?

Aware wa onaji
Katazato no
Ibuseki shizu ga
Fuseya ni mo
Tsuzure sasechoo
Kirigirisu
Hata oru mushi no
Koe goe ni
Awasu hyooshi no
Tooginuta.

Even in gloomy huts of the
    poor in one's own village,
We find beauty when grass-
    hoppers cry,
"Don your rags,"
Lovely is the chirping of the
    weaving bug,
In time to the clapping of
    distant falling blocks.

Ato-uta

Omoshiroya
Kureyuku mama no
Oozora ni
Kumanaki tsuki no
Kage kiyoki.

In the sky as it grows dark,
The bright penetrating moon-
    light is pure.
According to the ancients,
Such an evening is the glory
    of autumn.

Koyoi zo aki no
Monaka towa
Inishiabito no
Kotonoha o
Ima ni tsutaete
Shikishima no
Michi no shiori to
Nokoshikeru.

This is the guide in art
Which they have bequeathed to
    the people of Japan.
        (Shawn O'Malley, UCLA
        1967)

The lines of the uta of "Aki no Koto no Ha" retain the traditional lengths of 5 and 7 syllables, falling in alternation. The continuation of the long poem into the ato-uta prolongs the mood until the end of the composition.

A comparison of these five texts reveals both historical continuity and change. Continuity is seen in retention of the 5 and 7 syllable line structure.

Repetition of the last lines seems to have persisted also, though not as consistently as the line structure. The greatest change was in overall conception of structure.

In the kumiuta form of composition that preceded tegotomono, each of six songs was a separate and complete entity joined to the next by a brief instrumental interlude. This was the case in the kokingumi, as well, where the tanka in the "Chidori" and "Haru no Kyoku" mae- and ato-uta are all independent entities separated (or linked) by ai-no-te and by the tegoto. In the other compositions--"Saga no Aki," "Shin Takasago," and "Aki no Koto no Ha," however, the texts of the mae- and ato-uta together are conceived as a unified whole as is more usual in tegotomono.

When the ato-uta text continues and completes a mood or thought begun in the mae-uta, the conceptualization of the tegotomono compositions as a whole would appear to be different from that of kumiuta--a unified whole rather than a succession of self-contained sections. The tegoto would theoretically serve to enhance the mood by prolonging the tension as an integral part of the overall structure. The terms "mae-uta" and "ato-uta" themselves indicate a conceptualization of integration of the parts into a whole, the mae-uta being the "song before" and the ato-uta being the "song after" the central tegoto.

Setting of the Texts

Only for a moment or two in these uta do "purely melodic" considerations dominate the setting of the poetry; in fact, text and melody are complementary to

a remarkable degree. Only in "Saga no Aki" is the balance
different: the poetry is more important than melody.

The words and lines of the texts are set with care-
ful consideration to make them easily understandable and
to delineate the traditional structures of lines of 5 or
7 syllables. The means of achieving this are chiefly
rhythmic, through the use of rests, of relative durations
of syllables, of placement of syllables on certain beats.

Relatively few words are interrupted by rests either
between syllables or within a syllable. Most of the
broken words which do occur are four or more syllables
long, for example <u>shira 𝄽 mashi</u>, <u>furusa 𝄽 to</u>, <u>matsu 𝄽 ka 𝄽 ze</u>.

Indeed, for the most part rests notated in the vocal
melodies separate grammatical units or syllable units
(lines). In the "Saga no Aki" <u>mae-uta</u>, for instance, two
lines are set as demonstrated below.

Saga no 𝄽 atari no 𝄽   7 syllables

Aki no koro ≀𝄽   5 syllables

Translation: Saga no   atari no   Aki   no   koro
              Saga of   area of   autumn of evening

In Japanese the possessive "<u>no</u>" or "of" follows the word
to which it belongs; translated literally to English
these lines would read: <u>evening of autumn</u> <u>of the area</u>
<u>of Saga</u>. Translated more lyrically it reads "on autumn
evenings the area around Saga." Other grammatical units
are set off by "g<u>a</u>," "<u>wa</u>," "<u>ni</u>," as in "<u>oozora ni</u>," "<u>kiku</u>
<u>toki wa</u>."

In all these compositions use of rests serves to
subdivide most 7 syllable lines into 4 plus 3 syllables

or 3 plus 4 syllables, breaking between words or grammatical units. While some 5 syllable lines are subdivided
as well, most consist of one word or one grammatical
unit and thus are sung as an uninterrupted unit. The
third portion of the mae-uta text of "Aki no Koto no Ha"
(ms. 72-104) is given in Example 1 with the total duration devoted to each syllable placed below that syllable
and rests notated where they occur in the melody.

Example 1

In addition, a rhythmic pattern of relative durations is used to set off the beginnings of words or
grammatical units: a first syllable is assigned a
relatively shorter total duration than other syllables

in that word or phrase. Examples of this from "Chidori"
and "Saga no Aki" in Example 2 show the pattern in phrases
of both long and short words.

Example 2

Chidori <u>ato-uta</u>

I – ku – yo   ne – za – me – nu   7 syllables:
                                  setting off words

Su – ma   no   se – ki   mo – ri   setting off phrase

Saga no Aki <u>mae-uta</u>

Tsu – ki   wa   ku – ma – na – ki   7 syllables:
                                    setting off words

Shi – ba   no   to   ni   5 syllables:
                          setting off phrase

First phrases of the <u>mae-uta</u> (and of the first line
of the "Saga no Aki" <u>ato-uta</u>) tend to present an exception
to this general pattern, beginning as they do with a
relatively long duration, with the pattern of total duration of each syllable flexible after that point, as
demonstrated in Example 3.

Example 3

Chidori   Shi – o   no   ya – ma /

Saga no Aki   Sa – re – de – da – ni /

Aki no Koto no Ha   Chi - ri , so - mu - ru /

Shin Takasago   Ta - ka - sa - go   ya/

The rhythmic demarcation of words or grammatical units by rests and by a rhythmic duration pattern is complemented melodically, for most of those units are set in their own melodic unit distinguished by certain features. First, the initial two syllables of each unit are set to ascending melodic motion--which in itself is a type of stress. The ascent is usually one step or the interval of a third, but in both "Chidori" and "Haru no Kyoku" leaps of a fifth occur, and in "Aki no Koto no Ha" more than half the beginnings of words that were delineated with the short-long duration pattern were stressed with a leap up of a third, fourth, or fifth. Exceptions to this occur particularly in "Saga no Aki" where initial pitches are repeated more than in the other compositions; the melodic line in that composition is considerably more static and less rhythmically punctuated. These are all demonstrated in Example 4 (see brackets).

Example 4

Secondly, in all these five <u>tegotomono</u> except "Shin
Takasago" over half the pitches occurring on the long
duration of the short-long pattern are primary pitches
in the respective tuning: the base pitch or the pitches
at the interval of a fifth or fourth from the base pitch.
This was especially frequent in "Aki no Koto no Ha" and
"Saga no Aki." In Example 5 the syllables connected by
⌣ are set in the short-long pattern; the pitches on
which they are sung are given to the right. Base pitch
is "c."

Example 5

Aki no Koto no Ha

Aware wa onaji
Katazato no
Ibuseki shizuga
Fuseya ni mo
Tsuzure sasechoo
Kirigirisu
Hata oru mushi no
Koe goe ni
Awasu hyooshi no
Tooginuta.

In fact, those units which do not begin with a
primary pitch either end on one or eventually center on
one. The units from Example 5 which fall into this
category are those beginning "tsuzu," "sase," and "hyoo."
They are given in entirety in Example 6. For the most
part, then, these melodic units feature one of the
primary pitches of the tuning, and many of them appear
to be designed to move from one primary pitch to another,
as was the case in Example 4(c).

Example 6

Aki no Koto no Ha

Thirdly, an overall ascent to descent melodic shape
seems to prevail in each melodic unit--with exceptions,
of course. Those which ascend only or descend only or
are essentially static are usually combined with other
melodic units to form a larger ascent to descent shape,
but that will be discussed later. Each of the characteristics of melodic units that is mentioned above can
be seen in Example 9 of "Aki no Koto no Ha" and in the

complete transcriptions of these tegotomono.

Tegotomono melodies are notated in published scores
of the Ikuta tradition in groupings of 4 beats. (Occasionally a "measure" will consist of only 2 beats or
even 3, but by and large the grouping is in 4s.) Into
that quadratic framework are fit the lines of 5 and 7
syllables. The manner in which this is done is vital to
the style of tegotomono uta.

In "Chidori" and "Haru no Kyoku" the usual pacing
is for 1 syllable or 2 syllables to fall within each
4 beat grouping. In "Chidori" in which the most "florid"
uta melody is found, as many as 8 beats can be set to 1
syllable, but relatively speaking that is rare. In "Haru
no Kyoku" and "Shin Takasago" the irregular pacing of 1
and then 2 syllables per 4 beats lends a more fluid
feeling than the regular 2 syllables per 4 beats pacing
in "Saga no Aki." In "Aki no Koto no Ha" there are
occasionally 3 syllables in 4 beats followed by 1 syllable in the next 4. But in all these uta the prevailing
pacing is 2 syllables per 4 beats. See Example 7.

A change in the pacing of text syllables lends
rhythmic variety in the setting. In "Chidori," for
instance, the texture changes from prolongation of 1
syllable to more regular 2 syllables per 4 beats placement; see ms. 156-164 in the ato-uta contrasted with
the remainder of the ato-uta.

The pacing of syllables is complemented melodically
by another factor: the number of pitches sung to one
syllable. The styles of setting demonstrated in Example
5, for instance, are very different. The less syllabic
the setting is, the more "purely melodic" it is. In·
Chart 16 below the number of times a certain number of

Example 7

Chidori   1 syllable in 8 beats

Shi — o   no   ya —

[a] ————————————————— ma

Haru no Kyoku   Irregular Pacing

Yo   no   na ————————— ka —— a

ni   ta-e ——————— te

Saga no Aki   2 syllables to 4 beats

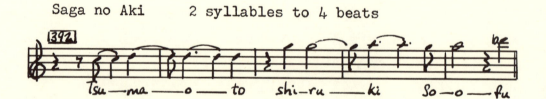

Tsu — ma —— o — to   shi—ru — ki   so—o—fu

Aki no Koto no Ha   3 syllables →1 syllable in 4 beats

Chi—gu—sa   ni

pitches were sung to a syllable is shown for each composition. Read across for the number of pitches per
syllable and down for the number of times that setting
occurred. "Saga no Aki" has the most syllabic text

Chart 16: Number of Pitches Per Text Syllable

Pitches →	1	2	3	4	5	6	7	8	9	11	12	14	17	18	22
Occurrences															
Chidori	32	18	15	6	5		3	1	3	1	1	1		1	2
Haru no	93	40	20	15	7	4	4	4							
Shin Takasago	42	19	6	3	4		1				1				
Saga no	89	8	11	4											
Aki no	124	53	23	16	12	6		1					1		

setting among these five <u>tegotomono</u>.
     But again, the style of setting might change with-
in a composition. Contrast the measures of the "Chidori"
<u>uta</u> given in Example 7 with the most syllabic phrase of
"Chidori" in Example 8.

Example 8

Chidori

The initial two syllables of many words and most grammatical units or lines are placed in one of the following fashions: 1) on beat 4 leading to beat 1; 2) on beat 2 leading to beat 3. This complements the short-long duration pattern that also occurs on those syllables, as is demonstrated by Example 9, the third portion of the "Aki no Koto no Ha" mae-uta. In the third and seventh lines, the settings of the words "shizu" and "mushi" eschew the short-long duration pattern, but are nevertheless placed on beats 1 and 3. The last line, being a last line of a mae-uta, would normally be performed with a ritardando; in this case the ritardando is also written into the melody. The setting is rather descriptive of the text, "tooginuta," "distant beating" ["the clapping of distant falling blocks"]. Example 9 is set up so that each new poetic line begins on a new staff line, but it reads continuously.

Within phrases the placement of syllables on beats is irregular. Example 10 is the fourth tanka in "Haru no Kyoku" mae-uta with the beat given on which each syllable is placed. The manuscript numbers indicate the second half of that beat, and slashes indicate bar lines.

Example 10

```
Ko - ma / na - be /- te
2   3    2    3     2

I /- za - mi / ni  yu /- ka /- n
4   1    3    1   4    1     2

Fu /- ru - sa /- to    wa /
4    1    3    1     3
```

Yu /- ki   to / ko - mi /- ko - so /
4___1   3   2___3   1   3

Ha - na / ya   chi /- ru - ra /- me /
2___3   2   4___1   3   2

Chart 17 shows the beats on which all syllables in these songs are placed, including the initial syllables. In "Chidori" beats 2 and 3 are most frequent; in "Haru no Kyoku" beat 1 has slightly more syllable placements; in the remaining three compositions beats 1 and 3 are most frequent. The overall picture is prominence of beats 1 and 3 for placement of syllables.

Chart 17: Placement of Syllables on Beats

Occurrences	Beat 1	2	3	4
Chidori	17	33	25	15
Haru no	55	43	43	40
Shin Takasago	34	23	33	22
Aki no Koto	65	52	78	41
Saga no Aki	34	23	33	22

Before assuming that this indicates the desire for rhythmic stress on beats 1 and 3, however, the off-beat or on-beat factor must be considered. Chart 18 gives the statistics for each composition; the manuscript numbers indicate the second half of the beat. In "Shin Takasago" and "Aki no Koto no Ha" the preference of the composers seems to have been to negate the prominence of beats 1 and 3 by placing syllables on the second half of those beats.

Chart 18:   Syllable Placement Within Beats

Beats	1	*1*	2	*2*	3	*3*	4	*4*	Total On-beat	Off-beat
Chidori	9	8	19	14	15	10	6	9	49	41
Haru no	28	27	22	21	18	25	13	27	81	100
Shin Taka	2	22	6	8	6	19	5	9	19	58
Saga no Aki	19	15	13	10	16	17	6	16	54	58
Aki no Koto	19	46	15	37	27	51	12	28	73	163

Off-beat placement is indeed very frequent; in fact, it is more frequent than on-beat placement in four of the five compositions. Chart 18 also gives the total number of on-beat and off-beat syllables in each composition. In the context of a strict structural organization of 5 or 7 syllables in a line, off-beat syllable placement tends to dim awareness of quantities, whether it is number of syllables or number of beats, but to enhance awareness of ongoing melody and rhythm. The setting seems appropriate for the poetry in which each line is linked to the next, with the thought completed only at the very end.

The melodic configuration of <u>tegotomono</u> <u>uta</u> as discussed thus far is one of a melodic unit for each word or grammatical unit set off by rests; most of those units initiated by ascending motion, either step- wise or a leap of a third, fourth, or fifth; about half landing on one of the primary pitches of the respective tuning. Using the same portion of the <u>mae-uta</u> of "Aki no Koto no Ha" as examined in Examples 5, 6, and 9, an- other aspect of melodic setting can be demonstrated:

longer phrases with a similar ascent to descent shape
created by linking of melodies of the single melodic/
grammatical units complement the on-flowing nature of
the text. The regrouping of the text units by melodic
movement is shown in Example 11 below; the melody is
given in skeletal form.

Example 11

Original Structure

Aware wa onaji
Katazato no
Ibuseki shizu ga
Fuseya ni mo
Tsuzure sasechoo
Kirigirisu
Hata oru mushi no
Koe goe ni
Awasu hyooshi no
Tooginuta

Melodic Restructuring

Aware wa
Onaji katazato no
Ibuseki
Shizu ga fuseya ni mo
Tsuzure sasechoo kirigirisu
Hata oru mushi no
Koe goe ni awasu
Hyooshi no tooginuta.

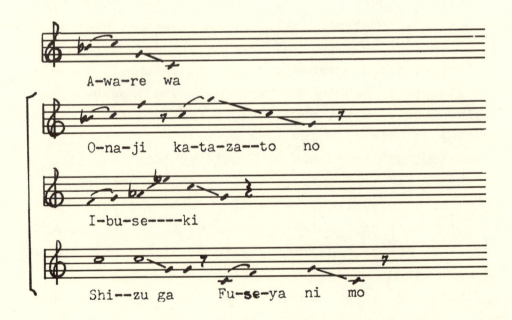

Tsu-zu-re   sa-se---cho-o   ki-ri-gi-ri---su

Ha-ta   o-ru   mu-shi   no

Ko-e   go-e   ni   a-wa-su

Hyo-o-shi   no   to-o   gi---nu----ta

FIVE / *Uta,* Part II: The Song and the *Koto* Composition

Uta in Tegotomono Form

The uta in tegotomono were the most traditional portion of the genre, in that most koto music and all shamisen music had theretofore evolved around song. What tegotomono offered was a new sharing of attention between song and instrumental solo. The balance between them varied from composition to composition as Chart 19 will show; the chart is arranged in chronological order for historical perspective. The number of measures in the uta include the transitions to the tegoto and the ato-biki.

Chart 19: Number of Measures in Sections

	Mae-uta	Tegoto	Ato-uta	Total Ms.	% Uta
Chidori	78	78	43	199	61
Saga no Aki	57	315	29	401	21
Aki no Koto	104	157	47	308	49
Shin Takasago	47	65	29	141	54
Haru no Kyoku	113	272	50	435	37

The mae-uta in each composition is longer than the
ato-uta, in number of measures, in number of poetic
lines and therefore in syllables (except "Chidori") as
shown in Chart 20. Relative proportions vary from
composition to composition, however. Lengths of mae-
uta vary more than lengths of ato-uta. The number of
measures in this chart exclude the koto transition and
ato-biki.

Chart 20: Lengths of Mae-uta and Ato-uta

| | Mae-uta | | | Ato-uta | |
	Lines/Syllables/Ms.			Lines/Syllables/Ms.	
Chidori	7	45	70	7	45	42
Saga no Aki	13	77	57	6	36	26
Aki no Koto	27	161	104	13	77	46
Shin Takasago	7	41	38	6	36	26
Haru no Kyoku	20	124	109	10	62	48

The events of a mae-uta section in tegotomono can
consist of a short instrumental introduction (mae-biki),
a song with koto interludes (ai-no-te), and a transition
to the tegoto played on koto after the song ends (tsunagi). The ato-uta may also include ai-no-te, and it is
usual for the koto to end the composition, even if only
with a few counts of melody beyond the end of the song
(informally called ato-biki). Charts 21 and 22 outline
the structures of the uta in these compositions.

Chart 21: Comparative Structures of the Mae-uta

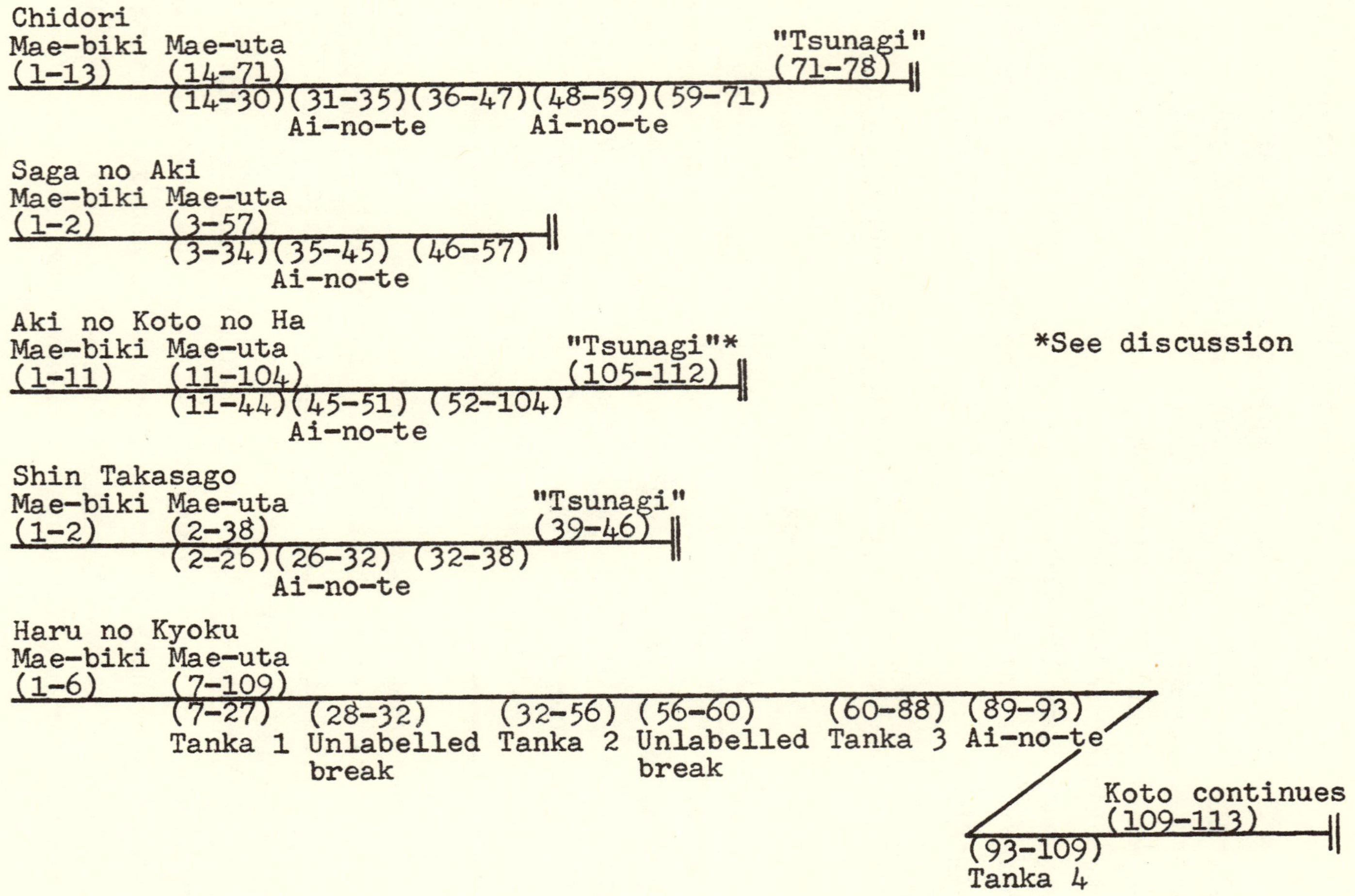

Chidori
Mae-biki   Mae-uta   "Tsunagi"
(1-13)   (14-71)   (71-78)
            (14-30)(31-35)(36-47)(48-59)(59-71)
                   Ai-no-te   Ai-no-te

Saga no Aki
Mae-biki   Mae-uta
(1-2)   (3-57)
            (3-34)(35-45)(46-57)
                  Ai-no-te

Aki no Koto no Ha   "Tsunagi"*
Mae-biki   Mae-uta   (105-112)
(1-11)   (11-104)
            (11-44)(45-51)(52-104)
                   Ai-no-te

Shin Takasago   "Tsunagi"
Mae-biki   Mae-uta   (39-46)
(1-2)   (2-38)
            (2-26)(26-32)(32-38)
                  Ai-no-te

Haru no Kyoku
Mae-biki   Mae-uta
(1-6)   (7-109)
            (7-27)(28-32)(32-56)(56-60)(60-88)(89-93) Ai-no-te
            Tanka 1 Unlabelled Tanka 2 Unlabelled Tanka 3
                     break   break

                                                Koto continues
                                                (109-113)
                                  (93-109)
                                  Tanka 4

*See discussion

Chart 22: Comparative Structures of the Ato-uta

Chidori
Ato-uta
(156-197)
(156-164)(164-171)(171-181)(181-187)(187-197)
Ai-no-te
"Ato-biki"
(197-200)

Saga no Aki
Ato-uta
(371-399)
(372-386)(386-392)(392-399)
Ai-no-te
"Ato-biki"
(399-401)

Aki no Koto no Ha
Ato-uta
(262-307)
(262-278)(278-281)(282-307)
Unlabelled break
(308 —)

Shin Takasago
Ato-uta
(112-137)
(112-124)(125-129)(129-137)
Ai-no-te
"Ato-biki"
(137-140)

Haru no Kyoku
Ato-uta
(386-437)
(386-407)(408-411)(412-437)
Tanka 5 Unlabelled Tanka 6
break
"Ato-biki"
(437-439)

Mae-biki

Each of these compositions begins with "foreplay" (mae-biki) on the koto, whether very brief as in "Shin Takasago" (one and one-half measures) and "Saga no Aki" (two measures) or more lengthy as in "Chidori" (thirteen measures), "Haru no Kyoku" (six measures), and "Aki no koto no Ha" (ten and a half measures). According to a note in the Sakamoto edition of the score, the mae-biki of "Saga no Aki" was added after the rest of the piece had been composed, so "Saga no Aki" must have originally begun with song as is more common in sankyoku compositions.

As shown in Chart 23 each mae-biki begins strongly with an octave on the base pitch or on the pitch at the interval of a fifth or fourth from the base pitch. These mae-biki consist primarily of emphasis on the strong pitches in the koto tunings through octaves and technical patterns. As shown in Chart 23 "Chidori" and "Saga no Aki's" mae-biki end on the pitch a fifth from base pitch, "Haru no Kyoku's" is on the fourth, and "Shin Takasago" and "Aki no Koto no Ha's" on base pitch.

The mae-biki begin the compositions in slow speed and with sparse writing. That of "Aki no Koto no Ha" is exceptionally melodic, but it is in character with the koto accompaniment throughout that piece.

Uta and Koto Accompaniment

In the preceding chapter it was stated that an over-all ascent to descent melodic shape seems to prevail in each melodic/grammatic unit—with exceptions, of course, and that a more prolonged ascent to descent shape is created by the linking of the melodies of the single units.

Chart 23: <u>Mae-biki</u>

The vocal ranges of the individual units vary considerably in "Chidori," from a third to an octave plus a third; in "Haru no Kyoku" from a second to an octave plus a second with no pattern discernable such as one of narrow range followed by one of more sweeping range.   In "Saga no Aki" with its many repeated pitches, the ranges are generally more restricted from a single pitch to a fifth; one phrase leaps an octave (m. 384). In "Shin Takasago" the units are of a single pitch to an octave, but most are a third to a seventh.   Those of "Aki no Koto no Ha" span from a second to an octave plus a third, but that uta has a relatively larger number of phrases an octave or more in range, as for instance, those shown in Example 1.   The total range required of a singer in each composition is given in Chart 24 below.

Example 1

Aki no Koto no Ha

Chart 24:   Vocal Range of Each Piece

Chidori	Octave + sixth
Haru no Kyoku	Octave + fifth
Saga no Aki	Octave + third
Shin Takasago	Two octaves
Aki no Koto no Ha	Octave + seventh

The overall melodic configuration of these <u>uta</u> is one of infrequent prolonged stepwise motion (in the Western sense), very frequent skips of a third, and fairly frequent leaps of a fourth or more. There is no instance in these <u>uta</u> of more than three consecutive half or whole steps (or combinations thereof) in descent or ascent; after three steps the melody either turns back on itself or proceeds to a leap. All of the instances of stepwise motion involving three or more pitches are enumerated in Chart 25. As the labelling of the pitches by <u>koto</u> string number and size of <u>oshide</u> shows, many of the instances include pitches other than those in the gapped tunings on the accompanying instrument. The chromaticism in "Saga no Aki" is unusual among these compositions, and it is remarkable in the light of the fact that the tuning of the piece eschews any half step. By and large, stepwise motion in these uta is created by the use of neighbor tones and is therefore restricted to two consecutive pitches.

The frequent skips of a third in the <u>uta</u>, however, are found in the tunings and in light of the fact that they occur on adjacent strings, the thirds should possibly be viewed as stepwise motion rather than as leaps in the Western sense. This would depend greatly on the

Chart 25:   Stepwise Melodic Motion

Chidori and Haru no Kyoku   Kokinjōshi

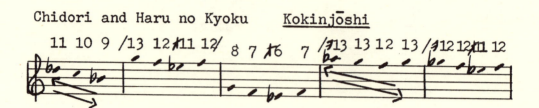

Aki no Koto no Ha
  Hirajōshi   Nakazorajōshi

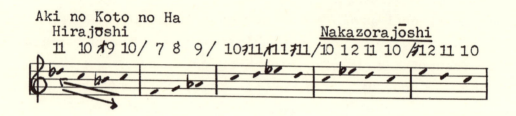

Shin Takasago   Takasago-kumoijōshi

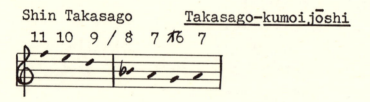

Saga no Aki   Unnamed chōshi

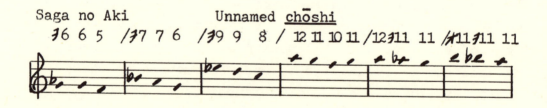

extent to which the <u>uta</u> melody pitches correspond to those of the <u>koto</u> tunings; this will be discussed in detail in the Conclusion.

Leaps of a fourth, more frequently of a fifth or sixth, even of an octave, occur within melodic units and

at the ends of melodic units.   These are often ascending
leaps which are then followed by a gradual descent.   See
Example 2.

Example 2

In <u>uta</u> melodies a leap up to a higher pitch register at a cadential point is sometimes used to minimize
the feeling of finality.   In "Haru no Kyoku," for example,
it occurred in the setting of the second <u>tanka</u>:   both at
the end of the 12 syllable segment and at the end of the
<u>tanka</u>.   See Example 3.

Example 3

5   Miyama ni wa
12   Matsu no yuki dani
     Kienakuni
14   Miyako wa nobe no
     Wakana tsumikeri.

Haru no Kyoku

In general, the koto accompaniments of the uta
melodies do not appear to follow the same pattern of
ascent to descent curve so consistently, although they
in fact do.   The shapes of the koto phrases are often
hidden by the use of those technical patterns idiomatic
to the instrument which lend considerable textural variety and create a more disjunct effect.   Ms. 91-96 of the
"Aki no Koto no Ha" mae-uta provide a good example of
this (Example 4).

The relationship of the uta and its koto accompaniment is for the most part heterophonic.   That is to say,
there are seldom two independent melodies occurring
simultaneously; the koto and voice complement each
other's melody.   This is not to say that the uta is
duplicated at the same moment on the instrument, for it
rarely is.   The pacing of the melody on the koto and in

Example 4

Aki no Koto no Ha

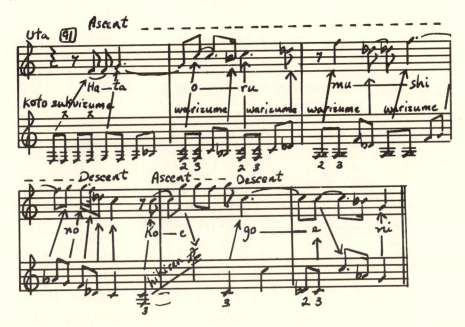

the song can be quite different.[1]

    As demonstrated in Example 5 the "Chidori" mae-uta begins with melismatic motion in the voice; the koto is given an outline melody which reinforces only the major pitches, anticipating them or playing simultaneously as they are sung. The accompaniment principle in both "Chidori" uta seems to be that when the vocal part is active the koto part tends to be less active. But during prolonged pitches in the vocal line, the koto is

[1] This supports Malm's definition of heterophony: multipart, each part rhythmically different but the difference caused by simultaneous variations on the same melody by each part (1972: 248).

assigned a more active role, often filling the prolongation with technical patterns that re-emphasize the vocal
pitch rather than distract attention from it.

Example 5

Chidori
End of <u>mae-biki</u> and beginning of <u>mae-uta</u>

In the "Chidori" <u>ato-uta</u> fewer melody pitches are
heard simultaneously from voice and <u>koto</u>. The pattern
of alternation that is prevalent in the other compositions takes precedent here. That pattern is demonstrated by a quote from the <u>ato-uta</u> of "Chidori" and the
opening <u>uta</u> measures of the other four compositions in
Chart 26.

Chart 26: Melodic Pacing in <u>Uta</u>
and Accompaniment

While the "Chidori" vocal part is perhaps the most "purely melodic" among these compositions with its melismatic phrases, its <u>koto</u> accompaniment is the most "patterned." Two descending motives occur many times, at cadences and within phrases:

Heavy use is also made of auxiliary tones and technical
patterns.

The koto accompaniment in the mae-uta of "Haru no
Kyoku" is like that in "Chidori." In Example 6 is shown
an instance when technical patterns keep the motion
going while emphasizing pitches in the song that are
being held for a long duration. The label "heterophony"
for the relationship between koto and uta in the last
three measures is questionable.

Example 6

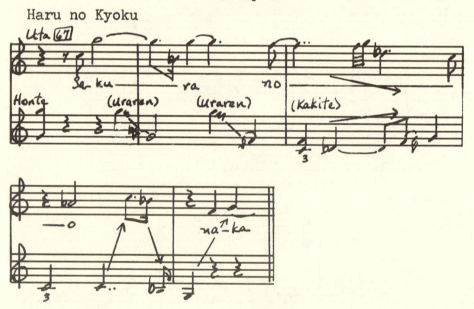

Haru no Kyoku

A kaede koto part was added to the ato-uta of "Haru
no Kyoku."[2] The second koto melody is complementary to
the song and to the honte koto part. While melodic

[2] According to Fujita (1934: 79) Matsuzaka Harue also
added a kaede to the "Aki no Koto no Ha" ato-uta accompaniment but it does not appear in the Ikuta score.

activity is certainly increased by the <u>kaede</u> at
moments, it does not function as an independent entity.
See Example 7.

Example 7

Haru no Kyoku

In "Saga no Aki" the heterophony between <u>koto</u> and
<u>uta</u> is exposed, with each melody note accounted for in
the accompaniment: the pitches are first sung, then
repeated on the instrument. The <u>koto</u> is not used as
frequently as might be expected to increase melodic
activity with a song that dwells on pitches through
long durations and repetitions. The <u>koto</u> melody becomes more active when the <u>uta</u> does. Both <u>mae-uta</u> and
<u>ato-uta</u> are accompanied by two <u>koto</u> parts, and the
<u>kaede</u> part is basically the same as the <u>honte</u>. In
Example 8 a relatively active measure is surrounded by
the more usual style of accompaniment.

"Shin Takasago" <u>uta</u> accompaniment consists primarily of the alternation of disjunct technical patterns
and melodic flow, the former during prolonged <u>uta</u> notes

Example 8

Saga no Aki

and the latter with active <u>uta</u>. The heterophony is a
clear alternation of pitches.

When the melodic skeleton is repeated in an <u>uta</u>, a
changed <u>koto</u> accompaniment can enhance the repetition.
Example 9(a) and (b) from "Shin Takasago" show the
nature of the <u>koto</u> to <u>uta</u> relationship in that composition, in addition to the manner in which slight differences can be made in basically similar material.

On the <u>koto</u> melodic descents of an octave span
occur in "Saga no Aki" and "Shin Takasago," but in "Aki
no Koto no Ha" they occur in ascent as well. And they
are expanded and expanded, even to a breadth of two
octaves plus a third. Beyond the opening measures of
"Aki no Koto no Ha" (which closely resemble those of
"Chidori") the melodic flow of the <u>uta</u> accompaniment is
unusually smooth. This is partially due to the absence
of a large number of disjunct techniques in the middles
of phrases. They are found primarily at the beginnings
of phrases and in the <u>koto</u> breaks. See Example 10(a),

Example 9

Shin Takasago

the opening measures of the uta, (b) well into the mae-
uta, and (c) near the beginning of the ato-uta.

In general, then, accompaniment of an uta begins
with a sparse koto part that underlines the principle
pitches of the uta—i.e. the melodic skeleton. As the
uta progress the voice and its accompaniment settle into
a pattern of technical patterns during prolonged uta
pitches, then both on melody particularly during descent
patterns. The relationship of voice and instrument is—
with some exceptions—heterophonic.

Example 10

Aki no Koto no Ha

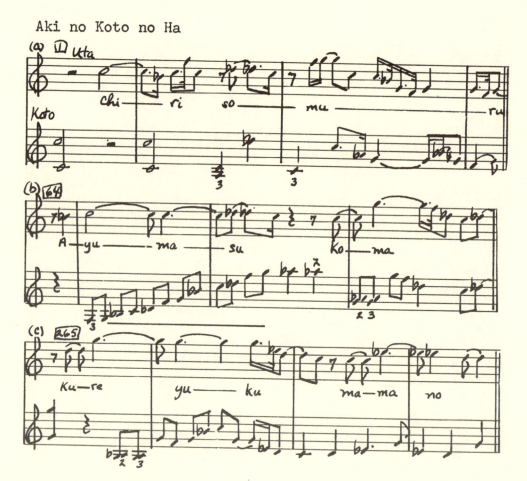

Ai-no-te

Ai-no-te, the solo koto passages between segments
of an uta, function primarily as transitions from one
segment to the next. In Example 11 is the first ai-
no-te from the "Chidori" mae-uta which shifts the base
from middle f to high f as a transition; like many ai-
no-te it retains the character of the koto accompaniment at the particular point in the uta--in this case,

Example 11

Chidori

sparse and with technical patterns providing only
skeletal melodic movement. Occasionally an ai-no-te
shifts the focus from the primary pitch on which a preceding phrase ended to the different primary pitch on
which the next phrase begins; see, for instance, "Haru
no Kyoku" ms. 26-32.

The second "Chidori" ai-no-te, which separates the
tanka from the repetition of the last two lines of the
tanka, is a literal repetition of the mae-biki. It is
the only instance of such repetition among these five
compositions.

Only in "Haru no Kyoku" and "Aki no Koto no Ha"
does an ai-no-te act as an end to one section rather
than as a transition between two; at the end of the
second tanka in the "Haru no Kyoku" mae-uta, for instance, the ai-no-te reiterates the fifth to base pitch

cadence which immediately preceded it and the third
tanka begins again at the fifth from base pitch with
only the subtle preparation afforded by the ato-oshi,
as shown in Example 12.

Example 12

Haru no Kyoku

In some ai-no-te where there are honte and kaede
koto parts the two instruments play almost the same
material, but in others they are relatively independent.
A good example of the latter is in "Shin Takasago"; see
Example 13.

Tsunagi

Only two of the five pieces have a tsunagi-type
section connecting the mae-uta to the tegoto: "Chidori"
and "Shin Takasago." In neither is the section labelled
tsunagi, but in the Ikuta score of "Chidori" there is a

Example 13

Shin Takasago Ai-no-te

remark at m. 73 that "some people say the tegoto begins
here." The sparse melody of the "Chidori" tsunagi lends
the feeling of finality with its cadential descent of an
octave and a fourth followed by an ascent to the pitch
a fifth from base pitch, with its general contrast to
what preceded it, and with the traditional ritardando
with which it is played. The tegoto then begins with a
strong unison on base pitch. The "Shin Takasago" tsunagi
consists of a long cadential descent of two octaves plus
a second, ending finally on base pitch.

In contrast, the "Haru no Kyoku" ending to the mae-
uta is a continuation of the phrase it follows. Without
pronouncements of finality, the melody just lands on base
pitch. "Saga no Aki" has only one beat of koto part beyond the end of the uta; both parts end on base pitch
together and the tegoto begins immediately.

In early editions ms. 105-112 of "Aki no Koto no
Ha" were marked as the beginning of the tegoto, but
in the 1971 Miyagi edition, it has been included as the
end of the mae-uta. The melodic writing is in contrast
to the built-in ritard at the end of the uta, however,
so this passage seems to be more an introduction to the
tegoto--therefore a makura--than a conclusion of the uta
section--a tsunagi.

Included in the <u>tegoto</u> sections in these compositions are the following subsections:

1. <u>Makura</u> and <u>mae-jirashi</u>--introductions to the
    <u>tegoto</u> proper.

2. <u>Tegoto</u>--the main body of this portion of the
    composition and the section which gives its
    name to the total form, <u>tegotomono</u>. It may
    consist of several sections, sometimes labelled
    <u>dan</u>.

3. <u>Hon-chirashi</u>--a final climax to the section,
    appearing in "Haru no Kyoku" as the second <u>dan</u>.

Within the structural framework of a <u>tegoto</u> there is
room for a good deal of variety and as the comparative
structural chart shows, no two of these are precisely
alike.

The <u>dan</u> in a <u>tegoto</u> proper are usually distinguishable from each other in performance by a decrease
in rhythmic density in the melodic movement, accentuated
by a ritardando on the part of the performer. The tempo
curve of the entire <u>tegoto</u>, then, is a relatively slow
beginning, a gradual acceleration within the first <u>dan</u>;
a ritardando to end each <u>dan</u> and consequent acceleration
in the next <u>dan</u>; a ritardando to make the transition

Chart 27:   Comparative Structures
of the <u>Tegoto</u>

Chidori

Section of Waves	Section of Plovers
(79-101)	(102-154)
22 ms.	52

Saga no Aki

Dan I	Dan II	Dan III
(58-131)	(132-249)	(250-372)
73	117	122

Aki no Koto no Ha

Makura*	Dan I	Dan II
(105-112)	(113-189)	(190-261)
7	76	71

Shin Takasago

Makura		
(48-57)	(59-113)	
	(59-88)	(89-113)
	29	24

Haru no Kyoku

Makura	Mae-jirashi	Dan I	Dan II
(114-136)	(137-161)	(162-307)	(308-385)
22	24	145	77

* In the most recent scores the <u>tegoto</u> is indicated
as beginning at m. 113.

into the <u>ato-uta</u> which begins without any formal musical
transition.

The "Chidori" <u>tegoto</u> was the only one among these
five compositions that was originally composed for solo
<u>koto</u> rather than for <u>honte</u> and <u>kaede</u> <u>koto</u>. It should
therefore provide a basis for comparison of composition
techniques for solo <u>koto</u> <u>tegoto</u> as opposed to those for
duo-<u>koto</u>. After discussing the "Chidori" <u>honte</u>, the
other <u>tegoto</u> <u>honte</u> will be examined in chronological
order of composition: "Saga no Aki," "Aki no Koto no Ha,"
"Shin Takasago," and "Haru no Kyoku."

"Chidori"

The "Chidori" <u>tegoto</u> is in two sections: ms. 79-101
labelled in the Ikuta scores "Section of waves" and
ms. 102-155 labelled "Section of Plovers" ("Chidori").
See Example 1 for the transcription of Section I arranged
to conform to the descriptive analysis below.

<u>Section I</u>. Following a <u>tsunagi</u> which ended the <u>mae-</u>
<u>uta</u> on the pitch a fifth from base pitch, Section I
begins with a strong unison (strings 2 and 7) on base
pitch (f). Then base pitch is re-emphasized by two
slightly different <u>hayakake</u> patterns in rhythmic diminu-
tion. In any tuning other than <u>kokinjōshi</u> this would have
emphasized the lowest pitch in the tuning on string 2.

Once base pitch has been firmly asserted the entire
range of the <u>koto</u> tuning is covered in one glissando
(<u>hikiren</u>), and two <u>hayakake</u> which parallel the earlier
ones reiterate the highest pitch on the instrument. The
rhythmic pacing in these two successions of events is
slow, spacious, and parallel.

Example 1

Chidori   "Section of Waves"

The rhythmic density increases abruptly at m. 85,
but the melodic content of the next twenty beats is a
reiteration of the <u>hikiren</u> content: the entire range
of the <u>koto</u> tuning is covered as all strings but number
3 are struck (plus the pitch obtained by a whole-step
<u>oshi</u> on string 11). The technical patterns employed are
<u>kakezume</u> and the octaves.

At m. 89 the activity centers finally on string 5,
sounding the pitch a fifth from base pitch, and remains
there for twenty-one beats. The rhythmic pacing of the
beginning of the section is repeated: spacious, then
with snowballing density as the <u>warizume</u> patterns are
shortened, resolving in m. 93 to a melodic pattern
common to <u>koto</u> music: ♩ .

Ms. 95-99 are a repetition a fifth higher of ms. 90-
94, with a slight difference in the final melodic resolution: ♩ . This unit centers on
pitch g (string 8); its lower octave sounds on string 3,
the only string which was not struck in the second unit
of this section.

Ms. 100 and 101 are the final cadence of Section I,
consisting of an ascent from g to c', a prolongation of
pitch c' (fifth from base pitch) through lower neighbor
tones and an octave pattern, and finally a return to
base pitch f.

Section I focuses on the entire <u>kokinjōshi</u> tuning
and in particular on its primary pitches f and c, and g.
It features parallel melodic and rhythmic structure, as
well as rhythmic contrast and development. In each unit
one or more technical pattern(s) is dwelled upon:

<u>hayakake</u>, <u>hikiren</u> and <u>hayakake</u>, <u>kakezume</u>, and <u>warizume</u>.

  <u>Section II</u>.   Section II is over twice as long as
Section I (52 measures to 22), but it contains many of
the same structural ideas. As shown by the skeleton
melody in Example 2, it begins with reiteration of the
base pitch, and the first large segment (ms. 102–115)
covers the range of the tuning from high a^b to c (fifth
from base pitch) through a long and gradual descent.
As the transcription in Example 3 shows, each smaller
unit focuses on one rhythmic pattern and/or one or more
technical pattern(s):

    Ms. 102–109 syncopation ♪♩ ♪ and <u>sukuizume</u>

    Ms. 109–113 ♫♩ , rhythmic snowballing and briefly,
            <u>ato-oshi</u>

    Ms. 113–115 ♫♩ , rhythmic snowballing, <u>warizume</u>,
            and <u>keshizume</u>.

M. 115 of <u>keshizume</u> serves to shift the melody back up
to the high register.

        Example 2

Chidori   Skeleton melody ms. 102–115

Example 3

Chidori   Ms. 102–115

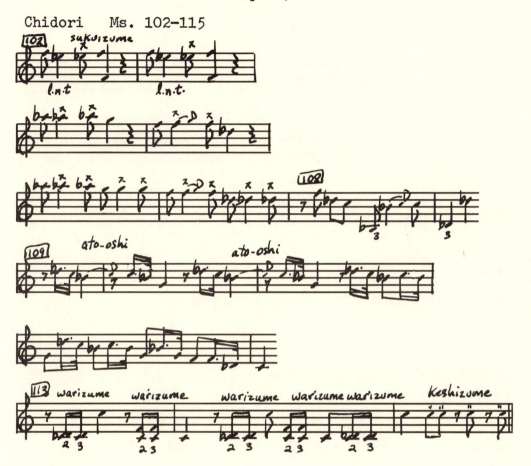

The skeleton melodies of the next large segments
are given in Example 4. A resemblance to the ascent to
descent curves of the <u>uta</u> can be seen in ms. 116–121;
the descent is to base pitch and again a technical
pattern takes the melody back up to the high register
for the next phrase. (See the complete transcription
for the full version.)

The reiteration of the tritone that is present in
<u>kokinjōshi</u> initiates the segment from ms. 121–132. The
melody does not begin to move again until the descent

Example 4

Chidori   Skeleton melody ms. 116-132

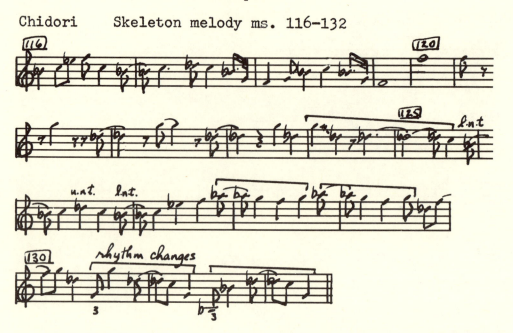

to c' is completed in m. 125. Due to the on-beat placement of the ♫ of the ♫♫ warizume pattern from ms. 125-
132, the pitches of the melody fall on the offbeat;
again there is a resemblance to the uta melodic practice.
Sukuizume, kakezume, warizume, oshiawase, and uraren
(sararin) techniques are all employed in these sixteen
measures.

And thus it continues until the last measures--
short motives repeated one after the other. In the last
three measures of the tegoto the rhythmic density decreases, and the performer ritards for a cadence, prolonging the pitch a fifth from base pitch with yet
another technique--the scraping surizume--before resolving to an octave on base pitch.

The "Chidori" tegoto is tightly organized rhythmically and melodically. It would appear that technical

virtuosity and variety were of prime consideration in
its composition.

"Saga no Aki"

The "Saga no Aki" tegoto is subdivided into three
sections, labelled dan in the Ikuta score, but the subdivisions are not indicated at the same points in the
Ikuta and Yamada scores. (See Chart 28). Where the
second Ikuta dan begins, however, a slight ritardando
is indicated in the Yamada score. Since the piece was
composed by an Ikuta musician, those subdivisions will
be the basis of analysis.

Chart 28: "Saga no Aki" Tegoto Structure

	Dan I	Dan II		Dan III	
Ikuta	(58-131)	(132-249)	(250		-372)

	Section I		Section II	Section III
Yamada	(58-	253)	(253-282)	(282-372)

The melodic emphases in the "Saga no Aki" tegoto
vacillate in a subtle fashion between g and d as base
pitches. Dan I begins on g base and ends on d; Dan II
begins on d and ends on the pitch a fifth from the d
base; Dan III begins and ends on g base. The internal
shifts are shown below in Chart 29.

When d is base pitch three melodic factors come
into play: 1) pitch e♭ is frequently present; 2) pitch
b♭ is used as well; and 3) the motive be-

comes prominent. The use of that motive is vital because it includes the primary pitches involved when

Chart 29:   "Saga no Aki" Tegoto
Harmonic Structure

Dan I

	m. 58	67	99	121		131
Honte	g base	d·	g	a (fifth	d	Ends on
Kaede	g base	d	g	from d)...i.e.d		d base

Dan II

	132	151	154	177	210	224	227
Honte	d base	settling		d	d	g Toward d/	a (fifth)
Kaede	d	momentarily				g d	from d
		on g					base

Dan III

	253	260	282		369
Honte	g	d	g also	d contd.	g
Kaede	g	d	important	d contd.	g
			due to		
			rhythmic		
			placement		

either g or d is base pitch: g and d, d and a. Pitch g
functions only as a lower neighbor tone to pitch a when
d is base pitch--unless it consistently occurs on strong
beats as around m. 282 where the three pitches are all
prominent.

Pitch e♭ is obtained by **half step oshide** on strings 4
and 9 on Koto I, strings 7 and 12 on Koto II. It is
used as a passing tone in descent from g to d, as an
upper neighbor tone (or appoggiatura) to d, and often in
an angular descending leap from pitch a down to d that
emphasizes the tritone a--e♭--d. See Example 5(a) and
(b).

Pitch b♭ is obtained by **half step oshide** on strings 7
and 12 on Koto I, string 10 on Koto II; although the
lower octave b♭ could be obtained on both kotos, it is

Example 5

Saga no Aki

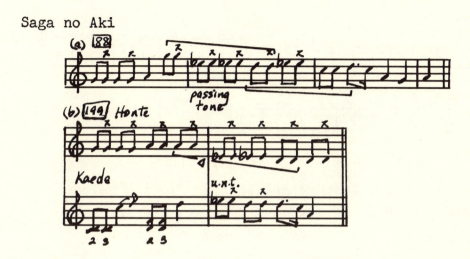

not used. Pitch b♭ occurs most frequently in descent:
. Both e♭ and b♭ thus provide most of the rare

instances in "Saga no Aki" when half steps are present
in the melody. Since no half steps occur in the tuning,
they must be created by <u>oshide</u>.

<u>Dan I</u>. As the "Chidori" tegoto began with an itera-
tion of base pitch and a display of the range of the
range of the tuning, so the "Saga no Aki" tegoto begins,
but the melodic means of doing those two things are very
different in the two compositions. Between ms. 58 and
75 the range from string 11, then string 713 (m. 61) down
to the lowest pitch (ms. 71-2) is covered, but with relatively little use of technical patterns. The melody
flows, for the most part following the consecutive strings
on the instrument. In ms. 74 and 75 a repetition an
octave higher takes the melody back up for the next unit.
See Example 6.

Example 6

Saga no Aki

In m. 76 the texture shifts from flowing melody to
rhythmic pulsation on repeated pitches, featuring the
sukuizume technique. (See Example 7(a).) Then after a
final bridge measure (90) of sukuizume, the writing
returns to being more melodic, but with some rhythmic
syncopating. In ms. 109-129 the octave technique pre-
vails (see Example 7(b)). The remaining ten measures in
the dan approach the cadence and keep within the high
octave d between strings 9 and 13. The cadence is the
descending pattern with pitch e♭:

Dan II. Dan II begins in a syncopated rhythm ♩♩♩,
ascending from d to a (strings 9 to 12). Then in m. 136
the sukuizume technique is used in the same rhythm as
shown in Example 7(a), but the melodic motive emphasizes
a tritone: . From ms. 144 to 183
the part is very active; sukuizume, octaves, lower
neighbor tone patterns, warizume follow in quick succession. Somewhat more attention is paid to the lower register of the tuning than in Dan I.

Example 7

Saga no Aki

In m. 184 the first indication is given that the
kaede part is necessary to the honte: 3 beats, then an
entire measure of rest is given to the honte. That never
happened in the "Chidori" tegoto where the longest period
of silence was 2 beats in Section I, 1 beat in Section II.
On the other hand, if m. 187 to 200 are considered a unit,
then the snowballing rhythm found in "Chidori" is found
here. See Example 8.

Example 8

Saga no Aki

In the remainder of Dan II the melody is less dense
rhythmically (though played faster) and relatively static
melodically. Sukuizume and octaves, repetition of the
pattern containing the tritone, and reiteration of the
primary pitches of the tuning provide most of the material. In fact, the kaede part contributes considerably
to the melodic and rhythmic interest in this portion of
the tegoto.

At ms. 183 and 249 in Dan II two beats are omitted
or could be omitted, truncating a notated grouping of
four beats. No interruption is caused by the omission.

Dan III. The honte part in Dan III is again more
active and its melody sweeps the range of the tuning.
Contrast, for example, the last measures of Dan II and
the beginning measures of Dan III quoted in Example 9.
Hardly any reference is made in the third dan to the
tritone motive featured in Dan II. At ms. 315—333 the
writing changes abruptly and again the continuity de-
pends on both honte and kaede parts; this instance is

Example 9

Saga no Aki

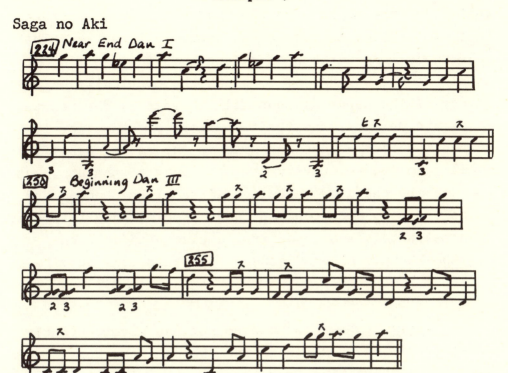

more extended than the one in Dan II. After m. 334 the
honte moves in ♩ ♩♩ syncopation and in steady beats,
following the pitches of the strings or jumping from
primary pitch to primary pitch.

The melodic structure of the "Saga no Aki" tegoto
is not as obviously organized into segments devoted to
one technique after another as the "Chidori" tegoto was.
Nor is rhythm developed in such a clear-cut segmented
fashion. The attention to shift of base pitch is also
unlike the writing in "Chidori."

Three factors in particular point to a dependence
of the honte part on the kaede in "Saga no Aki." 1) The
manner in which the honte melody stays in the upper

register for long periods of time (as in Dan I) suggests
that allowance might have been made for the lower-tuned
kaede to provide melody in the lower register. 2) The
relatively long periods of silence--as many as four and
a half beats, would tend to break the continuity of the
melody if the kaede did not fill it in. 3) The relatively static melody for extended periods of time, for instance the forty-eight measures at the end of Dan II, is
similar to the relatively static melody of the uta, but
the uta are the slow sustained parts of tegotomono and
there the koto accompaniment adds some melodic interest.
It appears that a second part is also needed in the
tegoto--in this case a kaede, to sustain melodic vitality.

"Aki no Koto no Ha"

Makura.   "Aki no Koto no Ha" has a very tightly
constructed tegoto section with two dan, the first introduced by a transition from the mae-uta. In the most
recent edition of the Miyagi Ikuta score the transition
passage is included in the mae-uta as an unlabelled
tsunagi and the tegoto is marked as beginning at m. 113,
but musically it was more aptly placed in the older
editions as a makura in the tegoto.

In the makura the entire range of hirajōshi is
covered, including pitches b♭ and e♮ created by whole-
step oshi on strings 9 and 11. As shown in Example 10,
octaves, kakezume, warizume, and a hikiren are all employed in the eight measures. Pitch f is emphasized to
the extend that the base pitch seems to be shifted from
the c of the mae-uta to f, but in fact the makura
presages the harmonic character of Dan I. The inherent
strength of both the fourth and fifth from base pitch in

<u>hirajōshi</u> is given full play here, as pitches c, f, and
g found on strings 1, 2, and 3 are equally important
primary pitches.

Example 10

Aki no Koto no Ha

The <u>honte</u> in "Aki no Koto no Ha" provides a good
example of the close tie of the basic melody of nineteenth-century <u>koto</u> music to the tuning to which the
instrument was set. In addition, the basic melody of
this <u>honte</u> is set forth clearly with little of the
octave displacement and fragmentation that were prominent in "Saga no Aki," and the various methods of prolonging the basic melody pitches are prevalent.

<u>Dan I</u>. The first phrases of Dan I are given in
Example 11 with skeleton melody on a staff above the
<u>honte</u> part. Reduced even further as in Example 12, the
melody can be seen to consist again and again of the
same ascents and descents, a veritable paucity of basic
melodic material. But the vocabulary of means to deal
with that material such as shifting rhythmic durations
through use of selected idiomatic technical patterns,
shifting points of stress through rhythmic placement and

Example 11

Aki no Koto no Ha

Example 12

Aki no Koto no Ha

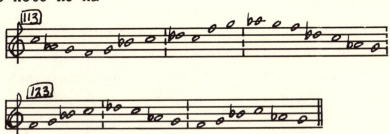

the like, is characteristic of <u>koto</u> music. See, for
instance, the contrasting settings of the same melodic
descents in Example 13(a) and (b) from Dan I. Further,
the handling of the vocabulary differed from composer
to composer, as each met the demand to provide variety
with clearly defined and rather limited means.

Example 13

Aki no Koto no Ha

As Dan I ends, the performer must slide the bridges
under strings 6, 7, 11, and 12 to the proper places to

shift the tuning from hirajōshi to nakazorajōshi. In
hirajōshi the descending passages to the primary pitches
were on the strings indicated in Chart 30. In nakazorajōshi those descending passages fall on different strings
causing the player to make a physical re-orientation. It
is an effective harmonic shift to g as base pitch. Because of the strength of the f-c axis in this dan in
hirajōshi, the shift is heard as a change of base both up
a step from f to g and from c to the pitch a fifth away.
The fact that both tunings have a strong string 2 (7 and
12, pitch g) in common probably accounts for the desire
of the composer to stress the c-f axis over the c-g axis
in Dan I in contrast with the g-c axis in nakazorajōshi.
The juncture measures are quoted in Example 14.

Chart 30: Descents to Primary Pitches
in "Aki no Koto no Ha"

Hira-
jōshi

Nakazora-
jōshi

Dan II. Dan II begins with clear affirmation of
the new pitch hierarchy--g as base pitch and d--by
sounding them simultaneously in the first beat and letting it sink in for a full four beats. Then within the
first thirty-two beats of the dan, all of the pitches

Example 14

Aki no Koto no Ha

of <u>nakazorajōshi</u> are used with the exception of those
on string 4 (but its octave 9 is present) and on strings
1 and 2 which were the strong pitches in <u>hirajōshi</u>.

The melody of the second dan is expansive in conception in that it covers the range of the tuning in flowing
sweeps. Rhythmically and melodically much of it appears
to have been planned to move constantly with motive
leading into motive, phrase to phrase practically without
stop. In Example 15 the sequence from ms. 198–219 is
presented, with brackets linking the motives; each is
numbered and explained below the example.

Example 15

Aki no Koto no Ha

1.   Octave descent begun by lower neighbor tone
pattern.

2.   Repetition of motive 1, beginning an octave
lower but reversing direction to end the same.

3.   Last 3 pitches of motive 2 repeated, then motive
extended by lower neighbor tone.

4.   Motive 3 repeated octave higher, using ato-oshi
to complete it.

5.   New motive, tritone leaving the descent incomplete.

6.   Completion of the descent, started higher and
encompassing 5.

7.   Further extension of the descent, reiteration
of 3 including lower neighbor tone.

8.   Repeat of lower neighbor tone, octave higher.

9.   Prolongation of the pitch d with

10.   Sukuizume technique plus reapproach to d an
octave lower, tritone leaving it incomplete.

11.   <u>Sukuizume</u> technique, and a resolution melodic motive completing the idea of 10.

12.   Repeat of melodic motive 11, extended to make pitch c a lower neighbor tone into 13.

13.   A parallel descent a fourth lower than 11 and 12.

14.   Repeat of 12 plus 13, an octave descent.

15.   Different form of 13 (or second half of 14).

16.   Repetition of last three pitches of 15, of octave descent extended by lower neighbor tone.

From m. 220 to the end of the <u>tegoto</u> in m. 261, the <u>sukuizume</u> technique, rocking octaves and then <u>wari-zume</u> emphasize rhythm as much as melody, but the seemingly incessant motion and the wide-range sweeps continue. The melody also continues to follow the pitches of consecutive strings on the instrument. In ms. 227-233, for instance (see Example 16), the writing is different from the measures quoted above, but the principles of organization are the same. Again, the motives are explained below the example.

Example 16

Aki no Koto
no Ha

1.   Melodic motive on consecutive strings: 12 11 12 13 (7 6 7 8).

2.   Parallel motive on consecutive strings: 10 9 10 11 (5 4 5 6).

3.   Descent from e♭ to d an octave lower on strings 12 11 10 9 8 7 6.

4.   An octave higher of what would have been a characteristic lower neighbor tone pattern at the bottom of the descent to d in motive 3.

5.   Repeat of 4 a fourth higher.

From m. 235 to about m. 249 the melodic base pitch seems to settle temporarily on c when a motive which starts out to be a characteristic descent ending in that lower neighbor tone pattern (g e♭ d c d), fails to return upward at the end, settling instead on the lower neighbor tone. (See Example 17.) Once more the lower neighbor tone proves to be an important melodic factor and variety has been obtained from familiar, often-repeated material.

Example 17

Aki no Koto no Ha

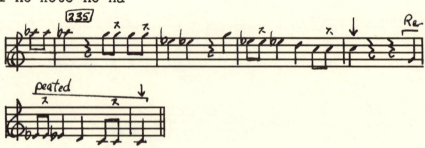

A final long descent of an octave and a fourth, performed with a considerable ritardando and ornamented

at the last with a scraping <u>surizume</u>, leads the "Aki no
Koto no Ha" <u>tegoto</u> to a close on a firm octave on d, the
pitch a fifth from base pitch. This <u>tegoto</u> <u>honte</u> would
seem to be able to stand by itself. That is to say, its
<u>kaede</u> part is undoubtedly complementary to it, but is
not as necessary as the <u>kaede</u> was to the "Saga no Aki"
<u>honte</u>. In fact, it seems as independent an entity as the
"Chidori" <u>tegoto</u> which originally had no <u>kaede</u>.

"Shin Takasago"

The "Shin Takasago" <u>tegoto</u> is the shortest among
these five compositions and is without formal subdivision.
It begins in a fashion now familiar, with an introductory
passage which emphasizes the strong pitches (a and e) and
covers the range of <u>Takasago-kumoijōshi</u>. As shown in
Example 18 the only string not employed in that introduction, ms. 48-57, is string 1 whose pitch is sounded in
any case on string 4; the three most frequent pitches
obtained through <u>oshide</u> are included--♯6, ♯11, and ♭13.

Example 18

Shin Takasago

It immediately becomes clear that this <u>tegoto</u> was
conceived for two instruments. Performance of the <u>honte</u>
without the <u>kaede</u> is not feasible because of the same
characteristic discussed for "Saga no Aki"--rhythmic and
melodic pacing. From ms. 58-67 (quoted in Example 19)
the writing for the <u>honte</u> is extremely sparse and disjunct. At ms. 85-87 another such moment occurs, nine
beats of rest in the <u>honte</u> where the melodic continuity
would be lost if it were not for the <u>kaede</u>.

Example 19

Shin Takasago

Between ms. 85 and 90 pitch d is momentarily the
base, calling into play string 1 with the interval of a
fourth on strings 1 and 2 that distinguishes this tuning
from <u>kumoijōshi</u>. The <u>kaede</u> reinforces pitch d strongly,
as shown in Example 20.

In ms. 68-83, on the other hand, and in the remain-
der of the <u>tegoto</u> the pace in the <u>honte</u> is constant motion,
covering the range of the tuning. The <u>sukuizume</u> technique,
<u>warizume</u>, and rocking octaves intermingle with flowing
melody in very clear motivic writing. The final sweep
into the <u>ato-uta</u> provides a good demonstration of this
(see Example 21). It ends in two descending passages

Example 20

Shin Takasago

that fall on consecutive strings, the first played out
in full, the second a <u>uraren</u> (<u>sararin</u>) glissando embel-
lished by <u>kasaneoshi</u>, concluding the <u>tegoto</u> on pitch e,
a fifth from base pitch, on which the <u>ato-uta</u> begins.

Example 21

Shin Takasago

This brief tegoto, then, was conceived for two parts and should not be played without both. It is a compact, very melodic composition that encapsulates traits seen in the previously discussed compositions: an introductory passage featuring the primary pitches and range of the tuning, contrasting rhythmic pacing, and use of familiar motives based on consecutive strings which are lent variety through idiomatic technical patterns.

"Haru no Kyoku"

Although "Haru no Kyoku" was one of the earliest of these five compositions, its tegoto was added late—in 1894 by Matsuzaka Harue. Matsuzaka apparently took the ai-no-te between the fourth and fifth uta to use as a transition (makura) into his Dan I (Fujita 1934: 11). In the Ikuta scores the internal sections of the tegoto are not labelled as explicitly as they are in Yamada score. The makura and mae-jirashi are clearly distinguishable musically, however, because the rhythmic density doubles at m. 137 and remains double until m. 157; in ms. 159-161 a ritardando is written in as the density decreases.

Chart 31: "Haru no Kyoku" Tegoto Structure

Ikuta	Dan I			Dan II
	(114	-307)		(308-385)
Yamada	Makura	Mae-jirashi	Dan I	Dan II
	(114-136)	(137-161)	(162-307)	(308-385)

Two factors suggest that while Matsuzaka might have used the original ai-no-te to begin the makura, he added

64 beats to it so that ms. 114-120 are probably Yoshizawa's writing and ms. 121-136 are probably Matsuzaka's.
The first factor is length: the rest of the ai-no-te
in "Haru no Kyoku" are 20 beats or less. The second
factor is more decisive: while Yoshizawa apparently
composed all of "Haru no Kyoku" in kokinjōshi, the tuning
of string 8 is to be changed (to b♭) at m. 121 and of
string 13 (to b♭') at m. 127. The new tuning is used to
the end of Dan I, but it must be changed back to kokinjōshi in Dan II to lead gracefully into Yoshizawa's
remaining two songs.

Between ms. 114 and 120 of the makura all of the
pitches in kokinjōshi are sounded, and whole-step oshide
on string 6 as well. In no other ai-no-te (or in the
mae-biki) did this occur. A glissando technique (sararin)
is also used, as is customary at the beginning of sections.
It is really remarkable that an ai-no-te originally written
to be tucked between the fourth and fifth songs would have
the characteristics of an introduction to a new section (?).

Ms. 121-136 establish the new tuning, as all strings
are sounded except string 1 which is doubled by 5, and
except string 3 (pitch a) which is no longer an octave
lower than string 8 and would disrupt the reinforcement
of the new tuning. In fact string 3 is used only three
times in Dan I by the honte and two of those times are
in a warizume pattern strings $[^2_3$ $[^2_3$ ⟶ 7. It is used
more frequently by the kaede--nine times, of which five
are the same warizume pattern. The base pitch remains f,
sounding on strings 2, 7, and 12; new prominence is given
to b♭, the interval a fourth from base pitch.

Both the makura and mae-jirashi are marked by
repetition of short melodic motives, in the same register

or in a different register, with the same melodic configuration or changed, as demonstrated in Example 22. At the
beginning of each new motive that is repeated is a circled
number; brackets indicate the melody involved in repetition.

Example 22

Haru no Kyoku

In motive 4 note that the intervals between the
first four pitches are repeated a fifth lower with the
help of an <u>oshide</u> on 6, while the descents in the last
three pitches follow consecutive open strings.   Note

also that one beat in m. 142 is optional; if the four-beat
groupings in the <u>koto</u> notation were conceived as metrical
in the Western sense (i.e. with strong pulsation on
beat 1) this would be quite disruptive, but obviously
that is not the case.

The writing in the <u>makura</u> and <u>mae-jirashi</u> is similar
to that in Yoshizawa's "Chidori" <u>tegoto</u>. It is particularly striking in such passages as those given in
Example 23. The succession of brief discrete motives,
most repeated and featuring a wealth of technical patterns is like "Chidori," unlike the more static style
in "Saga no Aki," and unlike the more flowing lines in
"Shin Takasago" and "Aki no Koto no Ha."

Example 23

Dan I. Since the <u>kaede</u> part begins in m. 162 of
"Haru no Kyoku" that point shall be considered the beginning of Dan I (as it is designated in Yamada score).
It starts in a compositional style similar to that of
the <u>makura</u> and <u>mae-jirashi</u>, consisting of a series of
units 16 or 18 beats long that are plays on change of
register, motivic repetition, question and answer, and
the like. A longer unit starts in m. 190 and the

difference is startling. Ms. 162-198 are presented in
Example 24 with each new unit beginning on a new staff
line.

Example 24

Haru no Kyoku

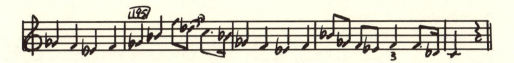

From ms. 198-208 occurs a passage where the melody
is broken up by rests; such a passage occurred in "Chidori" with only two beats of rest but this one extends
ten measures, too long to be sustained by a <u>honte</u> part
alone. It leads into an extremely virtuosic portion
(ms. 208-234), with <u>sukuizume</u> alternating with rocking
octaves in more extended lines and pulsating rhythm.
That is the pattern of succession to the end of the
dan: quick changes of pace with melodic fragments
giving way to on-flowing, wide-ranged phrases; short
units alternating with more extended ones, as sampled
in Example 25(a) and (b).

Example 25

Haru no Kyoku

From ms. 274-294 a technique associated with late
nineteenth century is used: a pluck with the middle
finger of the left hand (signified by 左). While this
technique did not appear in Yoshizawa's <u>tegoto</u>, it appears
here in conjunction with the snowballing rhythm that
occurred in the tegoto of "Chidori." See Example 26.

Example 26

Haru no Kyoku

<u>Dan II</u>. Dan I draws to a close with a built-in
ritardando that reiterates pitches g♭ and high b♭
(strings 8 and 13) in the last measures and ends firmly
on base pitch f. The tuning is changed during the

ritardando by the performer and Dan II begins with a
strong three-octave announcement that pitch g♮ and
kokinjōshi are again present. That transition is re-
produced in Example 27. Within the first 18 beats of
Dan II all the pitches of kokinjōshi are sounded, and
a whole-step oshide on string 6, as well. The glissando
technique customary at beginnings of sections is an
upward sweeping hikiren.

Example 27

Haru no Kyoku

Dan II is marked by rather constant motion and long
lines. But even within those long lines periodicity is
frequently noticeable more than, for instance, in "Aki
no Koto no Ha" where motive led into motive. In Example
28(a-d) passages are transcribed to show how even in
extensive phrases, segmentation can be felt. In (a) the
segments are of equal length and do not begin on beat 1.
(b) is an example of one of the few patches in this dan
where technical patterns predominate; included here is

the <u>keshizume</u> technique ("). Periodicity in (c) is
created in four measures more by the rhythm than by melody. (d) is a repetition of (c) an octave lower and is
the longest repetition found in these <u>tegoto</u>.

Example 28

Haru no Kyoku

This <u>tegoto</u> by Matsuzaka is a masterful combination
of the style of "Chidori" and the style of its late
nineteenth-century composer. Dan I is closer to "Chidori" but even in Dan II the approach to phrase structure

encompasses compact, shorter units within the wider-
ranged, longer units. The change of tuning is different
from "Chidori," but that had become common in tegotomono. The change back to the original tuning was unlike
common practice, but that was necessary in this particular instance. The use of one technical pattern after
another is not so systematically arranged in "Haru no
Kyoku" as in "Chidori," but they are employed extensively
to create a composition that is virtuosic and specifically idiomatic to the koto. In the days of Yoshizawa
Kengyō, this was probably a form of declaration of independence from the shamisen, and in the days of Matsuzaka
it was a desire to retain the spirit of the old composition but with the addition of a somewhat different
vocabulary.

Summary

These five tegoto show variety of formal structure.
That of "Shin Takasago" has no major subdivisions; those
of "Chidori," "Haru no Kyoku," and "Aki no Koto no Ha"
each have two; that of "Saga no Aki" has three subdivisions but the Ikuta and Yamada traditions do not agree
on their beginning points.

Most of the subdivisions begin with a clear melodic
statement of the pitch hierarchy and the entire range of
the tuning in which the particular composition is written.
Both sections in "Chidori" begin that way, as do Dans I
and III (Ikuta) of "Saga no Aki." The tegoto of "Shin
Takasago" is also initiated in that manner. The "makura"
of "Aki no Koto no Ha" covers hirajōshi, while nakazorajōshi is displayed at the outset of Dan II. The makura
of Dan I in "Haru no Kyoku" restates kokinjōshi in which

the <u>mae-uta</u> was composed, then affirms a new tuning for the <u>dan</u>; when <u>kokinjōshi</u> is used again for Dan II, it is reasserted in the first measures.

The ends of major subdivisions seem to be the only places in these <u>tegoto</u> where definite cadence points are discernable. Within sections the motion is continuous; jumping register to keep it going, changing to a new technique without pause, motive leading into motive or some other means is employed. That is not to say that periodicity is absent, because periodicity is created by motivic repetition, change of technical pattern, change of rhythmic motive, and other such means. A definite cadence point is usually marked in this music by gradual decrease in rhythmic density and thereby a built-in ritardando (or as in "Saga no Aki" a direction in the score to go "gradually slower") approaching descent patterns which lead to a relatively long duration of a primary pitch of the tuning, customarily sounded in octave or unison. These are demonstrated in Chart 32 which includes all of the decisive cadences in these tegoto. The "Saga no Aki" ends of both Dans II do not follow the formula, and this might be the reason for the disagreement over sectionalization in the Ikuta and Yamada traditions.

Chart 32: Section Cadences
in <u>Tegoto</u> <u>Honte</u>

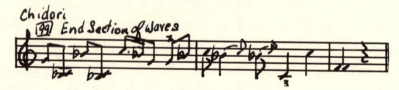

It appears that the rhythmic organization in "Chidori" and in "Haru no Kyoku" differs in one respect
from that of the other three compositions. Rhythmic
and melodic units of two beats, four beats or a few more
create an awareness of regular short-term periodicity
even in the context of longer phrases. Placement of
rests, repetitions of rhythmic patterns, transposition
of short melodic motives and other means contribute to
this. That rhythmic organization contrasts with "Saga
no Aki" where movement between and leaps between primary
pitches and neighbor tone patterns follow one another
to create an irregular periodicity with, for example, a
unit of three measures followed by one of thirteen, then

three, then seven, then four measures (ms. 102-135). It also contrasts with "Shin Takasago" and "Aki no Koto no Ha" where the melody just keeps going with scarcely any feeling of periodicity.

Several factors suggest that the rhythmic organization is a-metrical. The option to omit two beats, even one beat in a notated four (Ikuta) or two (Yamada) beat grouping makes it clear that a grouping of beats as they appear in notation is not intended to carry the connotations of meter. The absence of cadences marking off ends and beginnings in a metrical context is also a factor. In addition, the placement of the melody pitches on the weak halves of beats, particularly in disjunct technical patterns such as <u>warizume</u>, contributes to a lack of metric stress. This is similar to the off-beat placement of vocal pitches and syllable changes in the <u>uta</u>.

In all the compositions variety is achieved through contrasting rhythmic and melodic texture. Flowing, meandering melody (usually on consecutive strings) suddenly gives way to melodically disjunct technical patterns, and that to familiar short motives repeated in a different guise. With such constant clearly delineated contrast there seems to be little need for organization by phrases with cadences. In "Saga no Aki" the shifting of harmonic base is a further means of variety.

The <u>honte</u> in these <u>tegoto</u> must bear different relationships to their <u>kaede</u>. The "Chidori" <u>tegoto</u> was of course composed for solo <u>koto</u>, so the <u>kaede</u> is an overlay. The "Aki no Koto no Ha" <u>honte</u> can satisfactorily be played without the <u>kaede</u>; perhaps this is because it was fashioned after the <u>kokingumi</u>---therefore presumably after "Chidori" which was the only <u>kokingumi</u> with <u>tegoto</u>,

and that for solo <u>koto</u>. The "Saga no Aki" <u>tegoto</u> is
peculiarly static and it would appear that the <u>kaede</u>
part contributes considerable interest. In "Shin Takasago" and "Haru no Kyoku" the <u>honte</u> are independently
sustaining for the most part, but contain passages where
the <u>kaede</u> part is clearly meant to fit and needed to
maintain continuity. The <u>kaede</u> are discussed in the
chapter which follows.

SEVEN / *Tegoto,* Part II: The *Kaede*

Types of Honte-Kaede Relationships

In nineteenth-century koto and shamisen performance practice there were several different types of
relationships between honte and kaede.

1. An ornamental part to be played with a basic
melody.

2. Two equally interdependent parts played
together.

3. Two independent compositions or portions of
compositions, one previously existing and the other new,
played simultaneously (danawase) (Adriaansz 1973: 16).[1]

4. Two equally long dans of a tegoto played simultaneously, then again played as the performers exchange
parts (dangaeshi) (Adriaansz 1973: 16).

5. A second instrument on an ostinato (kinuta-ji)
(Kishibe Lecture Notes: Koto-4).

6. A second instrument reiterating and exploiting
the base pitch (sugomori-ji) (Kishibe Lecture Notes:
Koto-4).

[1]Malm (1959: 181-2, 168) explains danawase as "the
compositional process in which the basic koto (the honte)
plays a completely independent melody." Harich-Schneider
describes dan-awase: "The two parts proceed with all the
essential melodic parts in unison; but the unison is veiled
by opposite motion, suspensions, passing notes, and slight
rhythmical differences..." (1973: 520).

Early in the century in Osaka where the Ikuta
tradition flourished Ichiura Kengyō put ornamental koto
parts to basic shamisen melodies. Also in Osaka the
relationship was tried of equally important interdependent parts for koto and shamisen; such music was called
kaede-shiki sōkyoku (Adriaansz 1973: 16). It was among
Ikuta musicians in Kyoto that the kaede-shiki type relationship was most fully developed, however, under masters
such as Matsuura Kengyō (d. 1822) and Kikuoka Kengyō
(d. 1847), and Yaezaki Kengyō (d. 1848) who was most noted
for arrangements of numerous shamisen compositions.[2]

The most famous example of danawase, the simultaneous performance of two compositions or parts of those
compositions, is currently performed frequently. With
"Rokudan," the masterpiece of eighteenth-century danmono,
is played the first half of "Akikaze no Kyoku" by
Mitsuzaki Kengyō (d. 1853). Each is six dans long, with
each corresponding dan the same number of beats. In
addition, the styles of the two are homogeneous. The
remaining three types of relationships, dangaeshi,
kinuta-ji, and sugomori-ji, have not been as popular.

The fact that the kaede under consideration here
have no separate titles would suggest that they are not
compositions sufficiently independent to be performed
alone and that therefore they are not of the danawase
type. But it remains to be seen if they are ornamental
versions of the honte or if they share the kaede-shiki

[2]Arranged from Matsuura Kengyō were "Sue no Chigiri,"
"Wakana," "Uji Meguri," "Yotsu no Tami," and from
Kikuoka Kengyō, "Isochidori," "Chaondo," "Yūgao," "Fune
no Yume." (Fujita Tonan 1932: 454). Dates for Ichiura
Kengyō are not available.

type or relationship with equally important interdependent parts.

"Chidori." In the Ikuta score the kaede which
Matsuzaka Harue added to the "Chidori" tegoto begins at
the second subdivision, "Section of the Plovers." In
the Yamada score the kaede begins 48 beats before the
end of the first section (m. 90); the origin of those
additional measures is a mystery. The Ikuta kaede starts
as the tegoto (Section I) did, with a sucession of
technical patterns; here they stress the basic pitches
in the honte melody. The "Chidori" kaede remains very
close to the honte throughout, providing rhythmic contrast more than melodic.

A major means of providing rhythmic contrast in
"Chidori" is through kakeai, passages where the honte
and kaede play alternately, usually in imitation. This
can only occur where silence or sufficient pitch duration in the honte part permits; space was found in three
of those rhythmically snowballing passages mentioned
earlier (see Ex. 1 for one of them). In "Chidori" the

Example 1

Chidori   (Yamada Notation)

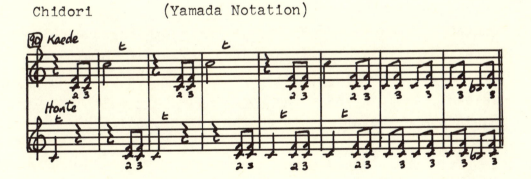

kakeai are brief but numerous (five). The most independent passage in the "Chidori" kaede is quoted in
Example 2; it, too, is very brief.

Example 2

Chidori

"Saga no Aki." The "Saga no Aki" kaede is an independently sustaining part; in fact, it is a far more
active piece of music than the honte and if it were not
for those passages (mentioned in the honte discussion)
where the periods of rest are long to permit an extensive kakeai, the kaede could probably be performed on
its own. As it stands, the honte and kaede have a kaede-
shiki type of relationship.[3] The relationship is an

---

[3] They are not kaede-shiki sōkyoku since that was a
term applied to koto-shamisen ensemble, but the type of
relationship musically is presumed to be similar.

equally important and interdependent one.

    The interrelationship is sometimes very subtle
as in Example 3. Also in ms. 135-139 the kaede part is

Example 3

Saga no Aki

extremely subtle in that  contains

both the honte motive and a motive of its own that is
repeated: 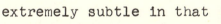 This passage is written out

in Example 4; it is the only instance in these five
compositions of a <u>kakeai</u> in which the <u>honte</u> and <u>kaede</u>
melodic motives are different. As usually happens when

Example 4

Saga no Aki

the two parts have been independent in some fashion, a
passage follows in which they are obviously related.

"Aki no Koto no Ha." The "Aki no Koto no Ha" kaede
is also an independently sustaining part. It is not,
however, as independent from the honte as the "Saga no
Aki" kaede was from its honte; it is far more consistently supportive of the honte melody. As Dan I begins
the two parts maintain fairly equal rhythmic density
(see Ex.5(a)), but as the dan proceeds the kaede frequently assumes the more active role, as in Example 5
(b) where for three measures it is an ornamental version of the honte. Example 5 (b) demonstrates as well
how the kaede part reinforces the cadences; this one
ends on Dan I.

Example 5

Aki no Koto no Ha

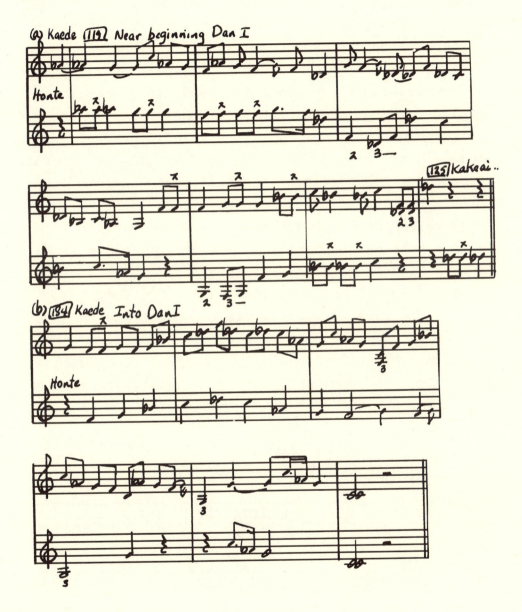

In this <u>tegoto</u> as in the others one part frequently anticipates the pitches of the other part, as
voice and <u>koto</u> accompaniment did in the <u>uta</u>; that can be
seen in Example 5.   In addition to anticipating shared
pitches in the context of relatively independent melody,
however, this <u>tegoto</u> includes four exceptional instances
where melodic motives are anticipated in a canonic
fashion.   In two of the instances the rhythm in the <u>honte</u>
and <u>kaede</u> differ, but in all the melodic motives are the
same.   In Example 6 (a-d) the four passages are quoted,
preceded by a synopsis of the motives in skeleton form.
In (b) the motive is repeated an octave lower by the
<u>kaede</u> while the <u>honte</u> extends the lower neighbor tone
pattern with which it ends; it is also a good example of
exploitation of octave displacement as a means to variety
and extension of a single idea.

The passages in Example 6 demonstrate the character of Dan II; both parts are constantly active with
scarcely a pause from beginning to end.   If a momentary
pause occurs in one part, the other usually plays across
the break.   It is a very exciting <u>tegoto</u>.

Example 6

Aki no Koto no Ha

"Shin Takasago." The "Shin Takasago" kaede is as dependent on the honte as the honte was said to be on the kaede. The kaede not only remains with the honte to a remarkable degree-- or on the same melody an octave apart due to the high-low tunings, but in one passage the honte and kaede even take turns carrying the melody. As shown in Example 7 this is different from the usual kakeai, because no melodic or rhythmic motives is split between the parts or imitated. A kakeai does occur in this tegoto and develops the snowballing rhythm first seen in "Chidori" (see Example 8).

Example 7

Shin Takasago

Example 8

Shin Takasago

"Haru no Kyoku." The "Haru no Kyoku" kaede has the
same type of relationship to its honte that the two parts
in "Aki no Koto no Ha" have: both independently sustaining parts with the kaede supportive of the honte
melody. Except for brief moments, both parts are
equally active throughout so that an already virtuosic
honte is complemented by an equally virtuosic kaede.
It is remarkable that the two do not detract from each
other, but that in itself is characteristic of honte-
kaede tegotomono; they are meant to complement, not
detract. The passage quoted in Example 9 should demonstrate that exceedingly well.

        For the most part the periodicity mentioned in
the honte discussion is maintained by the kaede, but in
several passages the kaede covers it with a longer
phrase or the two parts together make a longer phrase.
Three such instances are shown in Example 10 (a-c); in

(b) and (c) the lower neighbor tone is used to prolong
the resolution of the phrase.

Example 9

Haru no Kyoku

Example 10

Haru no Kyoku

The "Chidori" <u>kaede</u> part, then, is an overlay
that for the most part provides rhythmic contrast;
melodically the <u>kaede</u> is very close to the <u>honte</u>. The
"Saga no Aki" <u>kaede</u> adds considerable melodic and rhythmic interest to a relatively static <u>honte</u> and is so
independent of its <u>honte</u> that it approaches the <u>dana-
wase</u> type of relationship. The <u>kaede</u> and <u>honte</u> in "Shin
Takasago" are interdependent to a far greater degree
than in "Saga no Aki" because the <u>kaede</u> part is not as
self-sustaining. The "Aki no Koto no Ha" and "Haru no
Kyoku" <u>honte</u>-<u>kaede</u> relationships are similar; each
<u>kaede</u> is an active, independent part in itself, but
they both stay close to the <u>honte</u> melody. All of these
except "Chidori" are therefore examples of the <u>kaede-
shiki</u> type of relationship.

Details of the Honte-Kaede Relationships

Composers of tegotomono employed a considerable number of means to make the kaede complement the honte, yet have an individuality of its own. Found in these pieces are those listed below, all possible without the kaede departing from the original melody long enough to create a different skeletal shape.

1.   Different rhythm but same melody.

2.   Different technical pattern than the one played simultaneously by the honte.

3.   Melody where the honte has a technical pattern.

4.   A technical pattern where the honte has melody.

5.   Melody during rests in the honte.

6.   A technical pattern during a rest in the honte.

7.   Simplification of the honte melody, sometimes by use of technical patterns to emphasize only a few melody pitches.

8.   Same melody in a different octave.

9.   Octave where the honte has single melody pitch.

10.   Anticipation or following pitches in honte melody.

11.   Octave displacement in the middle of a passage in unison with the honte.

12.   Ato-oshi, passing tones, lower neighbor tones, or adjacent string tones added with a motive.

13.   Lower neighbor tone extension of a honte motive.

14.   Rhythmic alternation via technical patterns without creation of kakeai.

15.   Reversing the order of melody pitches.

16.   Exchanging octaves during motivic repetition.

17.   Swapping of motives.

18. One part on upper neighbor tone, other on lower neighbor tone.

Some of the writing in the kaede inevitably leads to changes in the skeletal melody. The ways in which this takes place in these compositions are:

1. Shifting of emphasis within the same selection of pitches.

2. Kaede and honte on different motives.

3. Motion carrying the kaede to a different octave adds to the skeletal melody.

4. Contrary motion.

5. Crossing of parts during contrary motion.

6. Resolution of a descent prolonged longer in kaede.

7. Resolution of a descent prolonged longer in the honte.

8. Reversal of order of segments of a motive (amplification of 15 in the first list).

9. Transposition of a motive so that the intervals are modified.

10. Kaede repetition overlaps with repetition in honte.

11. Kaede repeats part of a motive at the beginning of a phrase and catches up at the end of the phrase.

12. Repetition of kaede melody while honte proceeds to new materials.

13. Change in kaede melody while honte proceeds to new material.

14. Change in kaede melody while the honte reiterates a technical pattern.

Whatever differences there might be between the two parts within a melodic unit, the same periodicity

is generally maintained in both. In some instances the
<u>kaede</u> or <u>honte</u> begins or ends a beat earlier or later,
thus playing across a break, but they always come together again immediately thereafter. Exceptions to
this were pointed out in the "Haru no Kyoku" <u>kaede</u>, but
even they are few, brief, and resolved in the same manner.

 Repetition is an important organizational tool
in the manipulation of musical material in these compositions. Items 10-14 in the second list above involve
repetition of a non-imitative sort. While the <u>honte</u> repeats material the <u>kaede</u> sometimes repeats its own
material, repeats the same melody as the <u>honte</u>, or does
not repeat. Occasionally the <u>kaede</u> repeats melody not
shared by the <u>honte</u>. Change in figuration was shown to
be an important means of providing variety in repetition
of motives in the <u>honte</u> parts; likewise it is important
in the relationship between <u>honte</u> and <u>kaede</u>.

 Chart 33 on the following page summarizes the
repetition patterns in the five compositions and provides
further information on the relationships between the
<u>honte</u> and <u>kaede</u> in them. Since the number of repeti-
tions which occured in one part but not in the other is
small, relative to the total number of repetitions in
each part, the use of repetition would appear to be an
effective means of assuring homogeneity. The chart reflects a greater degree of independence in "Aki no Koto
no Ha" with its two very active parts, but it was pointed out earlier that even when melodic material is different the <u>kaede</u> is supportive of the <u>honte</u>. The unusual
degree of independence in the "Saga no Aki" <u>kaede</u> that
was discussed previously is confirmed here. The number

Chart 33: Repetitions of Melodic Material in the _Tegoto_

Number of Repeats in Honte Number of Repeats in Kaede

	Same Figuration	Different Figuration	Total	Same Figuration	Different Figuration	Total	Honte Only	Kaede Only
Chidori	14	1	15	15	1	16	2	3
Haru Dan I	8	9	17	.10	7	17*	2	1
Saga no Aki	20	2	22	10	10	20	8	6
Shin Takasago	2	3	5	3	2	5	1	1
Aki no Koto no Ha	14	7	21	16	3	19	6	4

*Eight repeats are not simultaneous with the _honte_ repeat; three are swapped with _honte_ repeats.

of times the <u>kaede</u> does not repeat when the <u>honte</u> does
is large, and when it does repeat the figuration is
different more often than in the other compositions.

The most obvious type of imitative repetition
in these pieces is <u>kakeai</u>. In these five compositions
there are nineteen; they occur only in the <u>tegoto</u> sections, but are not restricted to any particular section
of the <u>tegoto</u>. In "Chidori" they were inserted into
Dans I and II. In "Haru no Kyoku" they appear only in
the first <u>dan</u>, while in "Aki no Koto no Ha" they are
in both <u>dans</u>. The <u>kakeai</u> in "Saga no Aki" in both Dans
I and III are exceptionally extensive among these pieces.
In "Shin Takasago" there is one in the second phrase.

<u>Kakeai</u> are generally placed so as to introduce
a contrast in texture or a new melodic unit. Most are
preceded by brief introductions on the same melodic
material, but some begin outright. Fourteen of the
nineteen begin in the <u>honte</u> part with the <u>kaede</u> following in answer.

The relationship between the two parts with respect to similarity of motivic material and change of
pattern within one <u>kakeai</u>, varies greatly. The possibilities of this relationship are:

1. <u>Honte</u> and <u>kaede</u> on different technical patterns;
neither change.

2. On different technical patterns; the <u>kaede</u>
changes.

3. On different technical patterns; both change.

4. On different technical patterns; a long pattern is repeated.

5. On almost the same pattern; a long pattern is
repeated.

6.   On the same technical pattern; neither changes.

7.   On the same technical pattern; then the <u>kaede</u> changes.

8.   On the same technical pattern; first the <u>honte</u> changes, then both change.

9.   On the same technical pattern; both change.

10.   On the same technical pattern; both change the rhythm.

11.   On the same technical pattern; both change the rhythm and technical pattern.

Usually a pattern of one to three beats is repeated in alternation between the two <u>kotos</u>, but in three instances it was longer.

The <u>koto</u> part that initiates the <u>kakeai</u> generally initiates any internal change; an exception to this occurs in "Saga no Aki" where the <u>kaede</u> provides a descending motive to bridge between two portions of the <u>kakeai</u> (see Example 11). When the pattern changes within a <u>kakeai</u>, it is customarily both parts that change; in one instance in these <u>tegoto</u>, however, only the <u>honte</u> changed and in two other passages only the <u>kaede</u> changed. In "Chidori," "Haru no Kyoku," and also once in "Saga no Aki" (Example 11) the snowballing rhythm is used in <u>kakeai</u>. More often the rhythm is consistent, or changes and remains consistent thereafter.

In "Chidori," "Haru no Kyoku," and "Shin Takasago" the <u>kakeai</u> with one exception dwell on primary pitches, stressing rhythm rather than reiteration of melodic motives. One of the four in "Haru no Kyoku," however, divides an ascending major second between the two <u>koto</u> parts, and that is the interval which begins the melodic motive in the following passage. In "Aki no Koto no Ha"

three of the four have a melodic motive in the <u>honte</u>
to which the <u>kaede</u> responds with rhythmic embellishment.

Example 11

Saga no Aki

The "Saga no Aki" <u>kakeai</u> are distinctive: of
the five, two have the melody divided between the two
parts so that a motive is not complete without both
parts; in a third each <u>koto</u> repeats an ascending major
second; and in the remaining two <u>kakeai</u> each <u>koto</u> dwells
on its own melodic motive. The <u>kakeai</u> in Example 11

is one in which the melody is divided between the two
parts; that melody is "put together" in skeleton outline
in Example 12. This is a good demonstration of interdependence of the two parts.

Example 12

Saga no Aki ms. 185-195

The technical patterns used in the kakeai in
these compositions were warizume and kakite, sukuizume,
oshiawase, oshide and kasaneoshi, consecutive ascending
strings struck with the third finger, and left hand
plucking. The first three are by far the most frequent.

A further demonstration of the variety of vertical relationships between honte and kaede can be made
by charting the combinations in which one type of technical pattern was placed. In Dan I of "Aki no Koto no
Ha" the warizume technique was used frequently and as
listed below. The small letters in parentheses correspond to the pertinent events in Chart 34. Presumably
for further variety, warizume was scarcely used in
Dan II; (n) on the chart is from the end of it.

Chart 34: Vertical Relationships with <u>Warizume</u>

(a) Simultaneous with open octave in slower rhythm.

(b) Simultaneous with syncopation on upper string tone using same pitches as in <u>warizume</u>.

(c) Alternating with descending melodic motive.

(d) Alternating with <u>sukuizume</u> pattern.

(e) Alternating with the same technical pattern.

(f) Simultaneous with descending melodic motive.

(g) Alternating with rocking octave.

(h) Simultaneous rocking octave on a same pitch.

(i) Simultaneous with <u>keshizume</u>.

(j) Simultaneous with ascent on consecutive strings played by third finger, begun on same pitch and resolving together.

(k) Simultaneous with <u>sukuizume</u>.

(l) Simultaneous with <u>kakezume</u>.

(m) Emphasizing basically the same melody pitches, resolving together.

(n) Simultaneous with the same pattern, same octave or different.

When <u>warizume</u> meets <u>warizume</u> the effect is quite percussive. If they are in different octaves or emphasizing different pitches, momentary pitch clusters are created, such as those given in Chart 35. It is

important to emphasize, however, that even differing
technical patterns in the two parts usually emphasize
the same pitches in the basic melody.

Chart 35: Pitch Clusters

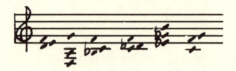

Octaves and unisons are formed by the meeting
of the two parts, but obviously a large number of other
vertical intervals are produced.   In descending order
of frequency, those intervals are:

1. major second.
2. perfect fourth, perfect fifth, minor seventh.
3. major ninth.
4. minor second, minor third, major sixth.
5. major third, perfect eleventh.
6. minor sixth, major seventh, minor ninth,
perfect twelfth.
7. augmented fourth, minor tenth, major tenth,
octave plus minor seventh, octave plus minor sixth.
8. two octaves plus major second.
9. diminished fifth, augmented eleventh, two
octaves plus minor third, two octaves plus perfect fifth.
The very wide intervals are formed in "Shin Takasago"
and "Saga no Aki" where the kaede is tuned to a lower
pitch register.   More than half the intervals formed
are the first three in the list and more than half of
the first three are seconds, sevenths, and ninths.

While the consecutive sequence in "Haru no Kyoku" quoted
in Example 13 is a bit unusual, such vertical intervals
are characteristic of this <u>koto</u> music.

Example 13

Haru no Kyoku

EIGHT / Conclusion

From a study of only five compositions, more can
be suggested than concluded, and that is the approach
of this final chapter. Here the parts are pulled together
to consider the whole, and elements which were isolated
for a close look are put into perspective. No attempt is
made to re-summarize the points of each chapter.

Relationship of the Parts in Tegotomono

It would appear that the kumiuta concept of organi-
zation--a succession of discrete entities--is replaced
in tegotomono by the concept of a unified whole, and
that the agent of unification is the song.[1] The poem
begun in the mae-uta, for example, is not complete until
the end of the ato-uta, and the pattern of alternation
of lines of 5 and 7 syllables in the uta continues from
the last line of the mae-uta to the first line of the
ato-uta. However, the customs of lifting a tegoto
from a composition to combine it with new song, or as
in the case of the kokingumi, of interjecting a tegoto
where none was originally intended, would suggest that
at least the tegoto was still considered a discrete

[1]For further study a comparison should be made of
kumiuta texts and text settings with those of tegotomono.
It appears that in kumiuta the formal structure of the
text could be irregular but the musical form is strict
while in tegotomono the texts are regular but the
musical form is not strict.

entity.   This is certainly the case today when it seems
to be permissable to perform the _tegoto_ of a composition
without the _uta_.

   While the texts of "Chidori" and "Haru no Kyoku"
were of an older origin than the others and were conceived as different types of poetry, the way they were
set was not appreciably different.   The style of setting
was found to be similar in these five pieces with respect
to the intimate relationship of grammatical unit to musical unit, and importance of the primary pitches of tunings.

   The relationship of the _koto_ accompaniment to the _uta_
is conceptually the same in all these compositions.   The
koto supports the _uta_, usually in heterophony, as
described in Chapter 5.   If there is a _kaede_ in the _uta_,
the _kaede_ takes the same role as the _honte_.

   Chart 36 shows the pitches used by _koto_ and voice in
each composition.   Only in "Haru no Kyoku" and "Aki no
Koto no Ha" does the voice part add pitches to the
repertoire.   In "Chidori" neither uses pitches additional
to the tuning that the other does not, and in "Shin
Takasago" and "Saga no Aki" the voice part calls for
fewer additional pitches.   It would therefore be possible for the instrument to accompany almost every voice
pitch if that were the desired relationship.   Since the
melodic style of the voice and _koto_ parts is so similar
and the repertoire of pitches equally confined in both
(indeed, both could produce more pitches than are used),
it is conceivable that at one time there might have
been at least the idea of the desireability of a one-to-
one relationship of accompaniment to song.

Chart 36: Repertoire of Pitches in Uta and Koto Parts

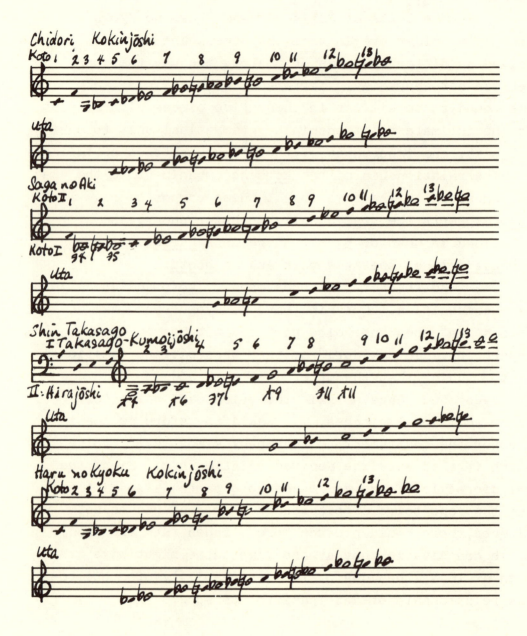

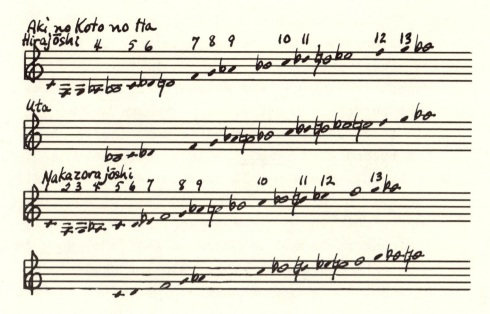

Another factor unifying tegotomono form is the
nature of the honte koto part. The writing for the
honte was found to be similar in uta accompaniment and
in tegoto. In "Chidori" heavy use was made of technical
patterns in both uta and tegoto in contrast with the
writing in "Aki no Koto no Ha" where the koto was assigned flowing melody from the mae-biki through to the
ato-biki, and in "Saga no Aki" where the honte koto is
relatively inactive throughout.

The relationship of the honte to the kaede in
the tegoto is not the same relationship of the koto
to the uta, however, and this is an important factor in
tegotomono. There is considerable variety in honte-
kaede relationships even within these five compositions,
but they can be reduced to two basic types: 1) a honte
that can stand alone without its kaede, as in "Chidori"
and "Aki no Koto no Ha"; and 2) interdependent parts
where both honte and kaede are necessary as in "Shin

Takasago."   "Haru no Kyoku" and "Saga no Aki" fit
into the latter type, too, but only because of the
extensive kakeai passages.

Except in danawase where two independent compositions are performed together, one melody in duo-
koto music is conceived as the basic part (honte) and
one as the second part (kaede). If a composition can
be played by only one koto, it is expected that it will
be the honte. In "Haru no Kyoku" and "Aki no Koto no
Ha," however, both the honte and kaede are practically
self-sustaining parts and in "Saga no Aki" the kaede is
close to being independent. This puts the kaede in a
different light and an hypothesis can be suggested for
future testing with a large selection of compositions:
as the independence of koto music from shamisen music
became more fully realized in the nineteenth century,
compositions for two kotos approached the danawase
conception even within tegotomono. Study needs to be
done, for instance, on the relationship between the
two koto parts in danawase, as compared to honte-kaede
parts in late nineteenth-century tegoto.

Because of the nature of the honte-kaede relationship in "Aki no Koto no Ha" and also because of the
style of the writing (see the summary of Chapter 6), it
seems that "Aki no Koto no Ha" was not composed in early
Meiji as sources suggest, but in late nineteenth century.
If it was indeed written after the form of the kokingumi, it seems likely that the kokingumi with honte-
kaede tegoto added were the model rather than "Chidori."

More Musical Factors in Tegotomono

The style of writing in these tegotomono is
based on the principle of constant variation within
the framework of a clearly delimited set of factors,
both melodic and rhythmic, by a clearly delimited set
of means, principally rhythmic. By and large, melodic
movement in both vocal and koto parts follows pitches
on adjacent strings on the koto, and therefore are "in
the tuning." Flowing movement over a number of strings
contrasts with brief motives of a few pitches that are
often employed repetitiously with different configuration. Melodic motives also include pitches created by
oshide, but even those usually lie on adjacent strings.
A few motives are disjunct, i.e. not on adjacent strings,
but the principle of composition is clearly not to invent
new melodies or exploit all inherent melodic possibilities.

In Chart 37 below the motives of each of these
five tegoto are given, introduced in each case by the
tuning from which they are derived. One of the few
means of melodic variation employed is to emphasize
different motives in each major subdivision of the
tegoto. Another means is to emphasize different pitches
within a motive.

Rhythmic variation in the tegoto is provided to
a great extent by the use of and the particular placement of techniques and technical patterns within a
melodic unit. Within uta sections rhythmic variation
is not developed as extensively because the song is
the most important element.

Chart 37:   Melodic Motives in the Tegoto

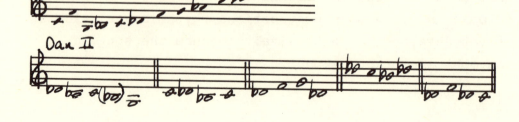

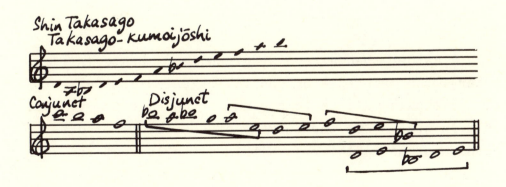

Aki no Koto-no Ha

Rather than a regular grouping by beats (as in meter), the principle of musical organization seems to be by melodic unit in <u>tegoto</u> and by melodic and textual unit in <u>uta</u>. (See the summary of Chapter 6 for discussion of periodicity.) Within a single beat the

orientation is duple subdivision. No triplet rhythm
was seen here, for instance, as it is in twentieth-
century compositions. In fact, the Ikuta system of
notation would not easily accommodate any subdivision
other than duple (and its multiples) because it is organized into boxes with the half-beats indicated by a
line half-way across the box. Nor do melodic units
fall into triple groupings of any sort.

Chōshi and Melodic Practice

Various sources assert that hirajōshi was derived
from the In scale. Adriaansz (1973: 34) explains that
it is the descending form of the In scale, as is demonstrated by Chart 5 in this study (p. 41). A close look at
the kokinjōshi intervallic structure reveals that it is
the ascending form of the In scale; see Chart 38 below.

Chart 38: Kokinjōshi and the In Scale

In his study of eighteenth-century kumiuta, Adriaansz
found that all the tunings used had the same interval
structure in the characteristic octave--that of hirajōshi;
therefore all compositions were in the same mode and all
changes of tuning within compositions were shifts in
pitch register.   In the tegotomono studied here, too, any
change of tuning within a piece retained the same mode.
As in kumiuta the tuning changes in "Haru no Kyoku" and
"Aki no Koto no Ha" are shifts in pitch register.

Furthermore, in "Haru no Kyoku" the inherent possibility of melodic variety at different pitch registers
within one tuning (see p. 32-3) was not exploited.   In
the second tuning the pitch of string 3 was no longer at
octaves from strings 8 and 13.   Instead of exploiting
that, string 3 was largely avoided.

In just the five tegotomono studied here, however,
three different modal structures are used:

Hirajōshi, Takasago-kumoijōshi,	
nakazorajōshi	S M3 T S M3*
Kokinjōshi and other "Haru no	
Kyoku" chōshi	T m3 T S M3
"Saga no Aki" chōshi	T m3 T m3 T.

This diversity would suggest that at least some degree of
modal variety was becoming desireable in nineteenth-century
composition for koto.

Oshide.   The oshide technique is used to add pitches
in the melody that are not present in the tuning; the tunings
are of the gapped type.   However, the gaps remain in the
scales obtained even with oshide pitches included.   The choic

*S is semi tone (half step); M3 is major third; T is
tone (whole step); m3 is minor third.

of additional pitches is obviously selective. It seems
likely that the reason certain ones are selected would lie
in melodic practice, the manner in which each is employed.

In all these compositions it appears that
pitches created by <u>oshide</u> are called into play mostly
in the context of primary pitches, i.e. base pitch or
the pitches at the interval of a fourth or fifth from
base pitch. Exceptions to this do occur, such as the
use of ↗7 and ↗12 in <u>kokinjōshi</u> and ↗9 (Koto I, or
↗12 Koto II) in "Saga no Aki." In Chart 39 the contexts of <u>oshide</u> in "Chidori" and "Haru no Kyoku" are
given as examples of this; the information is organized
according to primary pitch.

Chart 39: Contexts of <u>Oshide</u> in <u>Kokinjōshi</u>

A. Approaches to base pitch. (Tuning pitches ○)

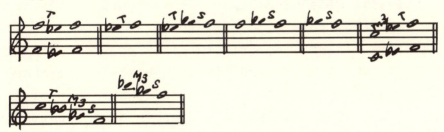

  1. Lower neighbor tone whole step.
  2. Lower leading tone whole step.
  3. Mordent whole step below, half step above.
  4. Upper neighbor tone half step.
  5. Appoggiatura half step.
  6. Ascent: m3 to whole step.
  7. Descent: whole step to M3 to half step.
  8. Descent: M3 to half step.

B.   Approaches to pitch a fourth from base pitch.

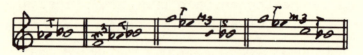

1.   Lower leading tone whole step.
2.   Ascent: m3 to whole step.
3.   Descent: whole step to M3 to half step.
4.   Descent: whole step to m3 to whole step.

C.   Approach to pitch a fifth from base pitch.

1.   Descent: whole step to m3.

        Several generalizations about melodic practice
can be made from this type of information from all five
compositions. First, no primary pitch of the tuning is
approached from a half step below; the lower neighbor
tones, lower leading tones, (and the lower pitch of a
mordent), and even the passing tones in ascent patterns
are at the interval of a whole step below. In "Saga no
Aki" an <u>oshide</u> (♯9 Koto I) was used to create a lower
neighbor tone to a non-primary pitch, but it is still
a whole step below.

        Secondly, upper neighbor tones and appoggiaturas
to primary pitches of the tuning are at the interval of
a half step above. The one exception to this in the
"Chidori" song is at m. 160, where the motion continues
in a descending pattern which, if it is resolved to
pitch c as customary, would be "in the style." But

since it does not, a tritone is outlined; this, too,
is "in the style:" . The tritone is

prominent in "Aki no Koto no Ha" and "Shin Takasago,"
as well.

Oshide upper neighbor tones are not as frequent
as lower neighbor tones in "Chidori," "Haru no Kyoku,"
and "Aki no Koto no Ha." In "Shin Takasago" there are
none, but in "Saga no Aki" they are more frequent than
lower neighbor tones.

Thirdly, motion between primary pitches is not
stepwise in the Western sense, although it could be
since the pitches necessary for stepwise motion are
used in other contexts. Instead, motion between primary pitches is determined by acceptable patterns of
ascent and descent and in either case involves a leap
of some size.

Whenever oshide pitches are needed to create
the desired patterns of ascent or descent, then they
are used for that purpose. Ascending motion between
primary pitches a fourth apart is by leap or by pattern; by far the most frequent ascent has the interval
structure m3-T.

Ascents of a fifth are more often by leap than
by connecting melodic movement in "Chidori" and "Haru
no Kyoku," but in the other compositions the reverse
is the case. The connecting patterns include oshide
pitches when needed. The interval structures of the
ascent patterns are enumerated in Chart 40; those
marked with an asterisk do not include the usual ascending fourth pattern and their occurrence in other
nineteenth-century compositions should be studied.

Chart 40:   Movement Between Primary Pitches
Using <u>Oshide</u> Pitches

Ascent of a 4th			Descent of a 4th		
Kokinjōshi and Haru no Kyoku chōshi	m3	T	Kokinjōshi and Haru no Kyoku chōshi	[M3 T	S m3
				m3	T
Aki no Koto no Ha			Aki no Koto no Ha		
Hirajōshi	m3	T	Hirajōshi	m3	T
	T	m3		[M3 T	S m3
			Shin Takasago		
			Takasago-kumoi-jōshi	M3	S
				T	m3
			Hirajōshi	m3	T
				T	m3
			Saga no Aki	M3	S

Chart 40 (Continued)

Ascent of a 5th			Descent of a 5th			
			Kokinjōshi and			
			Haru no Kyoku			
			chōshi	T	M3	S
				T	m3	T
Aki no Koto no Ha			Aki no Koto no Ha			
Hirajōshi	T	m3	T	Hirajōshi	T	M3	S
Nakazora-			Nakazora-			
jōshi	T	m3	T	jōshi	T	M3	S
	S	M3	T*	Uta	m3	T	T
			Koto	M3	S	T
Shin Takasago			Shin Takasago			
Takasago-						
kumoijōshi	T	m3	T			
Hirajōshi	T	m3	T	Hirajōshi			
			Uta	T	M3	S
			Koto	M3	S	T
Saga no Aki	S	M3	T*	Saga no Aki	T	M3	S

*Patterns unusual in these compositions

Descent patterns are more diverse. Descents of
a fourth between primary pitches are of three types:
T-m3, M3-S, and m3-T. Their occurences are listed in
Chart 40. The first of those patterns, T-m3, seems to
be a vocal pattern and is usually accompanied on the
koto by the M3-S pattern that falls on open strings; it
is demonstrated in Example 1 (a) from "Chidori." The
m3-T pattern is also demonstrated in Example 1 (a)
where the voice and koto are together in shifting the
harmonic emphasis to the fourth from base pitch. In
the "Haru no Kyoku" mae-uta Yoshizawa Kengyō displayed
two varieties of descending fourth in quite deliberate
fashion; see Example 1 (b).

Example 1

(b) Haru no Kyoku

Ki—e ——————— na——— ku

Descents of a fifth are for the most part
T-M3-S, with one exceptional T-m3-T in "Chidori."
These types are shown in Example 2 (a and b). In
"Aki no Koto no Ha" nakazorajōshi and "Shin Takasago"
hirajōshi a different distribution of intervals occurs
that should be studied in other nineteenth-century com-
positions--M3-S-T; see Example 2 (c). By frequency of
occurrence in all these compositions, however, it seems
that the T-M3-S descent of a fifth is the most desireable. Two generalizations can be posited from this
information about patterns of ascent and descent between primary pitches. 1) In ascent the preference
is to approach a primary pitch from a whole step or
more below, and in most cases (even in "Aki no Koto no
Ha") the distribution of the interval sizes in that
approach is [small-→large--small]. 2) In descent the
preference is not as strong. While upper neighbor tones
to primary pitches were seen to be consistently a half
step above, in descending from a fourth or fifth above,
the penultimate pitch is either a half or whole step
above destination pitch. While the distribution of
interval sizes in descent is usually [large-→
small-→large-→
small], there are those instances in "Aki no Koto no
small
Ha" and Shin Takasago" where the distribution is

large--small--small. <u>Oshide</u> is extremely important
for providing the pitches not present in the tuning
but which are needed for these patterns which are
characteristic of the melodic style.

Example 2

Returning to Chart 32 of cadences of major subdivisions of these <u>tegoto</u>, it can also be generalized
that at moments of finality, descent is preferred to
ascent, specifically descent from one primary pitch to
another a fifth below. Further, the descending pattern T-M3-S or a leap are most frequently present.

Oshide are also used in contexts which do not necessarily involve primary pitches of the respective tuning. In "Saga no Aki," "Aki no Koto no Ha," and "Shin Takasago" they are frequently the pinnacle or nadir of an ascent or descent. Instances of this are quoted in Example 3 a-c; (c) approaches the idea of non-patterned "pure melody" when a lower neighbor tone is used to approach a pitch other than a primary one.

Example 3

One further use of an <u>oshide</u> in <u>kokinjōshi</u>
occurs in both <u>uta</u> of "Haru no Kyoku" and of "Chidori." The melodic and rhythmic motive involved (see
Example 4 (a)) is particularly important, because more
frequent use of it is one major difference between the
versions of the songs published in 1967 and 1971.
Example 4 (b) compares measures from the 1971 Miyagi
edition of the "Chidori" <u>mae-uta</u> with those measures in
the 1967 edition. In the 1971 edition the motive
usually involves a tritone.

Example 4

Other than those melodic events pointed out for
particular investigation because they seem exceptional
among these five compositions, the melodic practices
summarized here conform to the ascent and descent forms
of the <u>In</u> scale. Those exceptional events occur primarily in "Shin Takasago," "Saga no Aki," and "Aki no
Koto no Ha" which might indicate a gradual change
through the nineteenth century in melodic practice, and
thereby in modal theory.

Epilogue

This study brings to the fore many questions that bear further investigation. For example, tegoto that far outbalance uta in tegotomono and the current practice of omitting the uta in performance raise the question: Why did the tradition of purely instrumental music for koto-- without song--remain relatively undeveloped until the present century? While the koto role in gagaku was to produce a "drone" (Harich-Schneider 1973: 194-5), Lady Murasaki mentioned in her eleventh-century Tale of Gengi a "modern virtuoso number on the thirteen-string koto" (Harich-Schneider 1973: 248). Whether or not that meant without song is not clear, but four centuries later the koto was being utilized as an accompanying instrument, replacing the wagon in fifteenth-century performances of vocal pieces (Harich-Schneider 1973: 411). Until Yatsuhashi Kengyo (d. 1685) "instrumental solos existed only in the form of preludes, interludes, and postludes to accompany vocal music" (Harich-Schneider 1973: 519). Solo danmono compositions of the eighteenth century were a significant but lonely development in this respect.

A common explanation for why the koto seems always to have been accompaniment for song is the strength of the literary tradition. But that is only a part of the story, it seems to me. Danmono did exist, after all, and remained in the active repertoire through the nine-teenth century, while compositions such as the kokingumi, which originally were all song with koto accompaniment, did not become current in that form. It would appear that an attitude toward conserving a tradition is a significant part of this musical phenomenon.

Such an explanation also should be considered for the question of why there continued for so many centuries the practice of utilizing less musical material than was

readily available on the instruments. For example, why
has melody remained tied so closely to the repertoire of
pitches and even the succession of pitches in the tunings?
Does this imposed restriction operate at all in other
Japanese arts, in other phases of Japanese life, and
if so, to what extent?

More work should be done on the types of musical
changes that were seen in the five compositions studied
here to see how the types of changes developed in the
late nineteenth century and early twentieth century before
the radical Western-type composition began. Does the
tendency found here for greater modal flexibility (as
manifested in new tunings) also appear in the types of
melody written? Is there less and less patterned,
motivic material and more and more flowing melody?
Is there an expansion of rhythmic flexibility to include
triple time? Are there compositions for instruments
alone, without the song whether performed or not? Does
the degree of homogeneity of musical style within the
repertoire decrease? If so, why? Do the same types
of changes appear in other Japanese arts and in other
aspects of Japanese life? If not, why?

Whatever the reasons, the koto is one of the
traditional instruments which has never lost its place
in the social and musical lexicons of Japanese history.
Tegotomono is part of a long and lovely tradition,
and maintains its place in musical time.

Appendix I. Notation and Publication of *Koto* Scores

The development of detailed notation systems
began relatively late in the history of <u>koto</u> music and
is an on-going process. The widespread use of notation
is very recent indeed. The information given here
supplements the material on the seventeenth and eighteenth century notations available in Adriaansz (1973:
Chapter IV).

A collection called <u>Chie no Hitoe</u> of 1833 was the
first to include the melody of the songs of <u>koto</u> pieces,
as well as the melody of the instrumental part.[1] The
<u>koto</u> notes appeared in large numbers, with the vocal
melody in smaller numbers. The pitches for the songs
were also notated according to the string numbers of
the <u>koto.</u> Songs are notated in this fashion to the
present day.

One reason why notation of scores and particularly
publication of scores came late was the possessive
attitude taken toward their musical tradition by the
blind artists in the Shoko-Yashiki (who obviously did
not use notation themselves). In 1837 near the end of
the Edo period, for example, Mitsuzaki Kengyō, the

---

[1]Most of the following information on notation and
publication of scores is from Tanabe and Yoshizawa (1963).

composer of "Godan Ginuta" and "Akikaze no Kyoku,"
published two collections of koto pieces, the Sōkyoku
Hifu (Secret Pieces) and the Genkyoku Gaihansho.
Since those collections included compositions considered secret by the guild, Mitsuazki was expelled for his
audacity. The style of the notation of those collections was basically that of the Sōkyoku Taiishō of 1779
which is discussed in Adriaansz.

The Meiji Restoration of 1868 had a decided effect
on the publication of koto music. When the Shoku-
Yashiki was abolished by law in 1871, koto music was
freed from the restrictions of the guild, and there was
a flurry of notating and publishing in both the established cipher system and in notes. The Music Bureau
of the government experimented with an international
notation and edited the Sōkyokushu in 1888. The same
year a private citizen, Umeda Isokichi, published
Gakuri wa Seiyō, Kakyoku wa Nihon, Ongaku Hayamanabi
(Western Theory, Japanese Melody, and a Shortcut to
Learning Music). His notation became standard for
Western-style Japanese notation of later years.

After the Restoration there were four major editions of koto scores: 1) those of the Kyogaku school
in Kyoto; 2) those of the Dai-Nihon Katei Ongakukai (an
association of musicians); 3) those of the Seiha
Hōgakukai (another association of musicians) and 4) those
of the Hakushindo Publishing Company which still pub-
lishes Yamada pieces. The Dai-Nihon association sponsors
two Ikuta editions which are particularly popular at
the present time, one of them the Miyagi Michio tradition
and the other a system developed by Sakamoto Goro.

Hogakusha Publishing Company prints the Miyagi editions,
as well as the Nakanoshima Kinichi editions of Yamada
pieces.

The preference of associations of musicians for
one style of notation over a selection of others per-
sists to the present and sustains the custom of non-
standardization. Yamada scores are notated in hori-
zontal lines to be read in the Western fashion from
left to right. The most popular Ikuta edition (Miyagi)
is notated in vertical lines, read in the traditional
Japanese fashion from top to bottom, right to left.
The Yonekawa edition of Ikuta pieces uses the horizon-
tal arrangement of Yamada scores. Miyagi Michio's
son edits yet another style of Ikuta score with the
melody given both horizontally as in the Yamada school
and in Western five-line staff notation. A sampling
of these styles is given in Example 1(a-d) of "Saga no
Aki."

When there are two (or more) _koto_ parts, they are
lined up vertically in the Yamada arrangement, with
the _honte_ on top and in darker print (see Example 1c).
In the Miyagi style of Ikuta notation the _honte_ is
given in full; then either the _kaede_ is given in full
by itself, or the entire _honte_ is repeated and lined up
beside the _kaede_.

In the Yamada scores the song is given in _honte_
tuning pitches. In the Miyagi edition of Ikuta scores
the song is given in _honte_ tuning pitches, then again
in _kaede_ pitches with the _kaede_ score if there is a
kaede in the _uta_ accompaniment. If the _kaede_ is in a
different tuning from the _honte_, the _uta_ pitches will
have been given according to two different tunings.

Example 1

(a) "Saga no Aki" Ikuta _ryū_ Sakamoto Edition of
Dai-Nihon Katei Ongakukai, published by Hōgakusha.

String Numbers

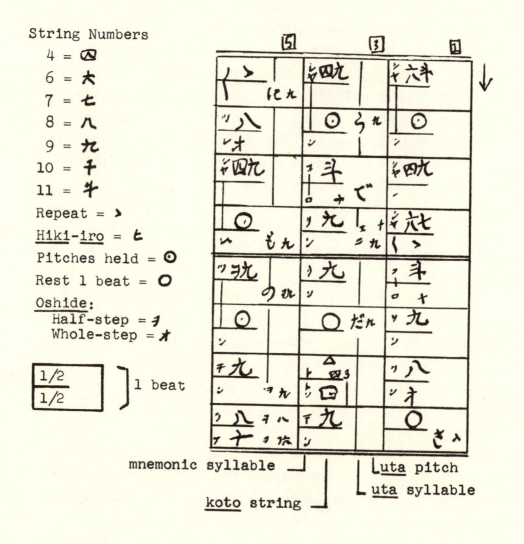

mnemonic syllable ⌐
koto string ⌐
ᒻ uta pitch
ᒻ uta syllable

(Example 1 continued)

(b) "Saga no Aki" Yamada ryū Nakanoshima Edition
published by Hōgakusha.

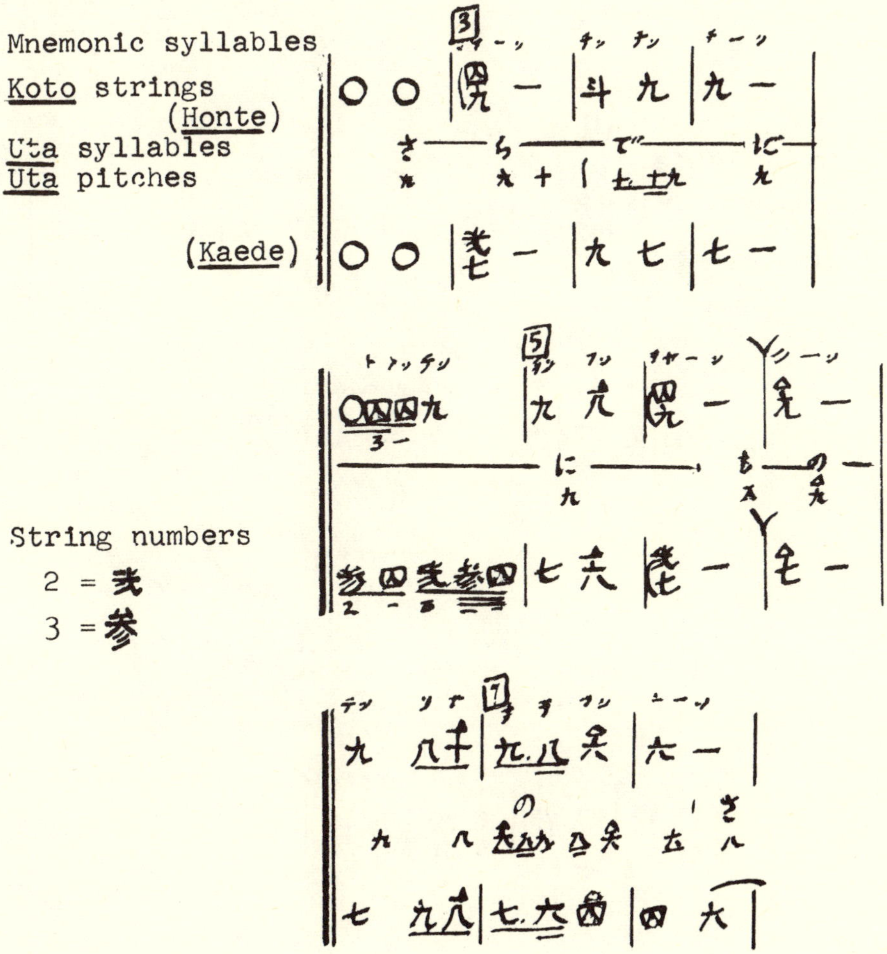

Mnemonic syllables
Koto strings
        (Honte)
Uta syllables
Uta pitches

        (Kaede)

String numbers
  2 = 弐
  3 = 参

(Example 1 continued)

(c) "Saga no Aki" Yamada ryū Hakushindo Edition.
Note the absence of a notation for the uta melody.

Mnemonic syllable
Koto strings
Uta syllables

(Example 1 continued)

(d)   "Saga no Aki" Ikuta ryū Yonekawa Edition
published by Sochokai.

Koto strings

Uta syllable
Uta pitches

さ　ら　で　だ　に　も　の
sa　ra　de　da　ni　mo　no

Other differences than graphic layout distinguish
Ikuta from Yamada notations. Yamada is more more
precise rhythmically than Ikuta. Many of the symbols
for techniques differ, as shown by the sample in
Example 2.

Example 2

Yamada   Ikuta

Yamada	Ikuta		
v	⅄	sukuizume	(backstroke)
△	⅃	oshide (raise the pitch one-half step)	
▲	⼂	oshide (raise the pitch a whole step)	
▲	⼂(大)	ato-oshi (raise the pitch a whole step after striking)	
▙	∧	kasaneoshi (lower the pitch after striking to release oshide)	

Some slight changes are made in different printings
of scores. In the 1971 printing of the Miyagi notation
of "Haru no Kyoku," for example, the following changes
had been made from the 1967 printing. In the uta slight
differences in rhythm occurred: ♪♫♫ to ♪♫♩ or ♫
to ♪♩ . In the makura ♫⎮♫ was changed to ♫ ⎮ ♪♪.
In the tegoto a consistent change was ♩.♪ revised to ♩.
Substitution of a rest for a prolongation or vice versa
would be crucial in the performance from notation only
if some means were intended for lengthening or shorten-
ing the duration of sound. However, since no such means
is called for and thus the decay time of the pitch is

not to be controlled, the rhythmic notation is arbitrary.
The _sukuizume_ technique was eliminated in several instances: ♫♫ on the same pitch throughout was changed
to ♫♫ with 6 and ↗5 the same pitch (see ms. 339,
362, 374).   In the 1971 printing of "Aki no Koto no Ha"
similar changes were made from the 1966 printing:
♪♩ ♪♫♫ changed to ♪♩ ♪↗♪♫ ; ♩♫♩ to ♩♫♩ .

Appendix II. Transcriptions

The notated differences in the Yamada ryū and Ikuta
ryū traditions of these five compositions are relatively
few and very subtle. "Chidori" includes the largest number
of differences. In order to provide an example of the
types of divergencies that exist between the two traditions
in compositions they share, an Ikuta ryū score of "Chidori"
is transcribed completely here, while the differences in
a Yamada ryū score are given. For the other four compositions only an Ikuta ryū version is given.

In the instrumental parts the Yamada differences
are of four types: durational and rhythmic; melodic;
ornamental; and technical. In the first category be-
long such details as rhythmic difference in the playing
of the same melody notes, with more dotted-note values
in the Yamada, or different value given to an ato-oshi.
Fermatas are utilized in Yamada scores at the ends of
sections where the pace has slowed. The Yamada version
occasionally adds two beats of rest or omits beats that
are marked optional in the Ikuta score.

The details of melody which are changed in the
Yamada tradition rarely affect the basic melody in the
original composition. The melody is sometimes simpli-
fied by the omission of passing tones; a few different
notes modify the direction of the melody temporarily;
the repetition of a pitch is omitted; an octave is struck

instead of a single pitch; or passing tones are added
to fill in a leap in the Ikuta melody. In "Haru no
Kyoku" the Yamada kaede koto part ceases before the last
poetic phrase of the ato-uta.

The differences in ornamentation are of three
types: a melody pitch played without an Ikuta embellishment; an ornament added to a pitch which was notated
without one in the Ikuta score; and a different ornament
than the one notated in the Ikuta score. The ornament
omitted is usually an ato-oshi. The ornaments added are
primarily ato-oshi, hiki-iro, tsuki-iro, and kasaneoshi;
relatively few such ornaments are notated in Ikuta
scores. The ornaments which Yamada players substitute
for those of Ikuta are tsuki-iro for ato-oshi, yuri-
iro for kasaneoshi, and ato-oshi for kasaneoshi. The
differences are subtle.

The greatest difference between the Yamada and
Ikuta versions of these pieces lies in the uta. Possible
explanations for this are that the uta were not notated
as early as koto parts and even today do not appear in
some scores, and that the styles of vocal music have
always been a point of distinction between the two
traditions. This subject calls for an exhaustive comparative study.

The transcriptions of "Haru no Kyoku," "Shin
Takasago," and "Aki no Koto no Ha" included here are
the 1971 printings of the particular Ikuta scores, up-
dated from the 1967 versions transcribed in the original
thesis. "Saga no Aki" appears here as it was in the
thesis. Details on the transcriptions are enumerated
below.

The starting pitches for the transcriptions were taken from the specified shakuhachi pitches. Measure numbers given in boxes are based on the Ikuta grouping of four beats even in the Yamada version of "Chidori." In the Ikuta scores certain beats are marked "optional," referring to adjustments necessary when the composition is performed with a player of either the Tozan or Kinko school of shakuhachi playing. Ato-oshi are indicated by smaller notes, with the stem turned in the opposite direction from that of the pitch on which they are based. They are connected by ⌒ to that pitch and given half the durational value unless it was otherwise indicated in the score: ♪. The numbers "2" and "3" are notated below pitches to be played with the index or second finger of the right hand.

Table of symbols:

▲	Yamada symbol directing the player to make an oshide, then release it in quick succession.
·· or 1)	Tsuki-iro technique, similar to the above.
/\	releasing of oshide.
۱۱	Keshizume technique, producing a twang.
←	Chirashizume technique, producing a swishing sound (Yamada ヅ).

Surizume technique, producing
a scraping sound (Yamada ←—→).

Backward flick technique related
to _chirashizume_.

Sukuizume technique, a backstroke
(Yamada ∨).

Uraren (_sararin_) technique, a
fluttering downward glissando
begun on string 13.

Hikiren technique, an upward
glissando.

Nagashizume (_kararin_) technique,
a flowing downward glissando.

Hiki-iro technique.

Left hand pluck.

Quick, ornamental pitch.

Oshide a whole step.

_Ai-no-te_.

Trail up successive strings with
third finger of right hand.

Chidori no Kyoku

Yoshizawa Kengyō

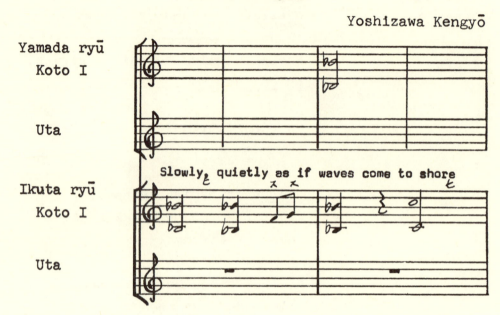

Yamada ryū
Koto I

Uta

Ikuta ryū
Koto I

Uta

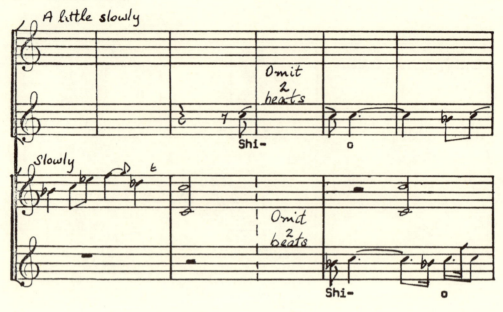

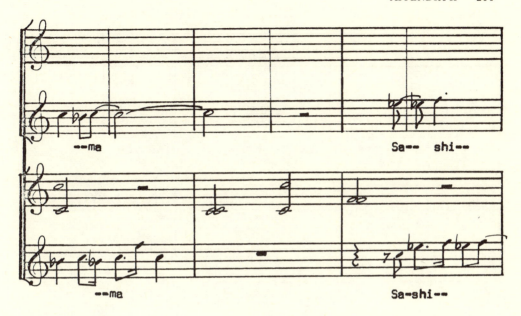

--zo   na-- ku

--zo   na-- --ku

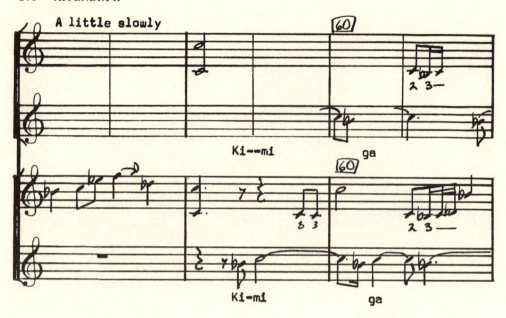

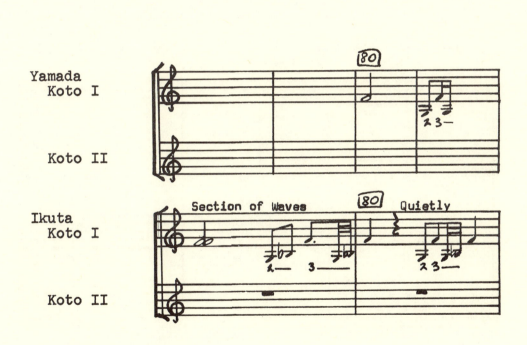

Little more slowly

Yamada
     Koto I

Uta

Ikuta
     Koto I

Uta

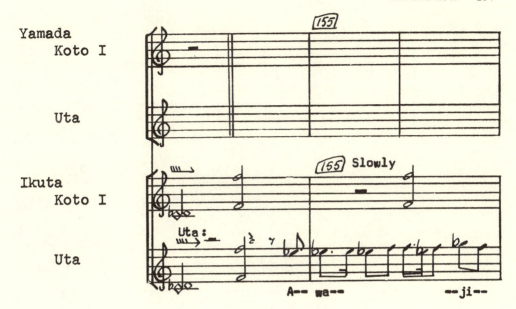

Saga no Aki

Kikusue Kengyō

Ikuta ryū
Uta

Koto I

Koto II

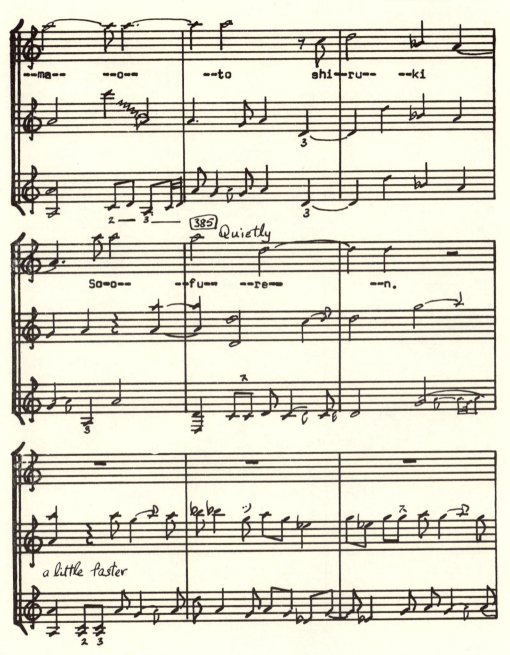

Aki no Koto no Ha

Nishiyama Kengyō

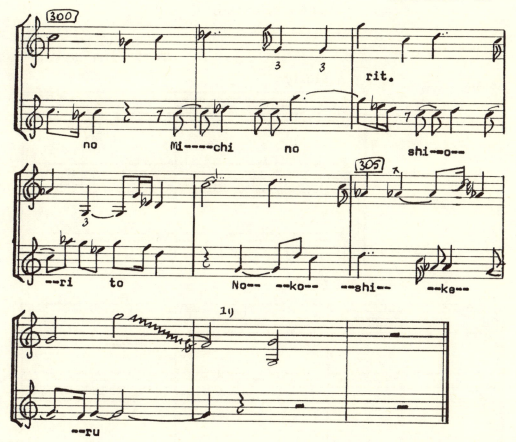

Shin Takasago

Arranged by
Terashima Hanano

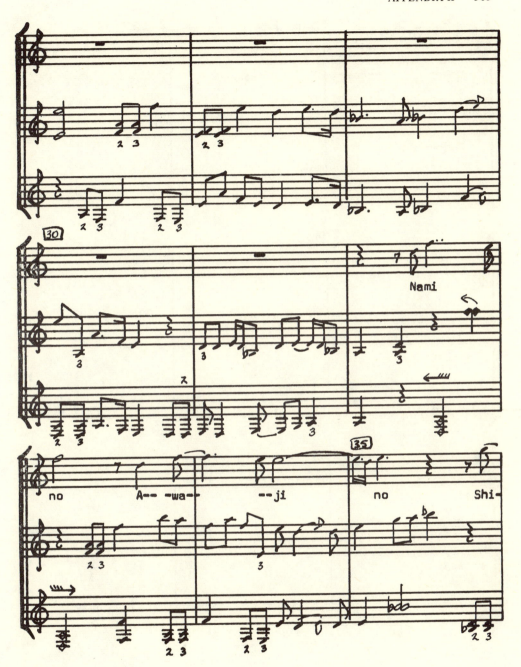

Haru no Kyoku

Yoshizawa Kengyō

Bibliography

Adriaansz, Willem Rudolf C.
 1967   "Research into the Chronology of Danmono,"
         Ethnomusicology, 11: 1, pp. 25-53.

 1968   "On the Evolution of the Classical Instrumental
         Repertoire for the Koto," Proceedings of the
         Centennial Workshop on Ethnomusicology,
         University of British Columbia, Vancouver.
         Victoria: Government of the Province of British
         Columbia, pp. 68-78.

 1970   "A Japanese Procrustean Bed: A Study of the
         Development of Danmono," Journal of the Ameri-
         can Musicological Society, 23: 1, pp. 26-60.

 1971   "The Yatsuhashi-ryū: A Seventeenth Century
         School of Koto Music," Acta Musicologica, 43:
         fasc. I-II, pp. 55-93.

 1972   "Midare: A Study of its Historic Development."
         In Kikkawa Eishi Sensei Kanreki Kinen Rombunshū
         [Festschrift for Professor Kikkawa Eishi].
         Tokyo.

 1973   The Kumiuta and Danmono Traditions of Japanese
         Koto Music. Berkeley: University of Cali-
         fornia Press.

Bonneau, Georges, ed.
 1934   Texte Intégral du Kokinshū. Paris: Librairie
         Orientaliste Paul Geuthner.

Brower, Robert H. and Earl Miner
 1961   Japanese Court Poetry. Stanford: Stanford
         University Press.

Dickins, Frederick Victor.
 1906   Primitive and Mediaeval Japanese Texts.
         Oxford: Clarendon Press.

Eckardt, Hans
   1957   "Japanese Music," Die Musik in Geschichte und
          Gegenwart, 6, pp. 1720-1754.

   1958   "Koto," Die Musik in Geschichte und Gegenwart,
          7, pp. 1646-1650.

Fairbank, John K., Edwin O. Reischauer, and
          Albert M. Craig
   1973   East Asia: Tradition and Transformation.
          Boston: Houghton Mifflin Company.

Fujita, Reiro
   1932   "Existence of the Yamada School and its
          History." In History of the Tozan School,
          Chapter 7, Part 4, pp. 469-478.

Fujita, Tonan
   1932   "A Brief History of the Transition of Sōkyoku
          and Jiuta." In History of the Tozan School,
          Chapter 6, Part 3, pp. 446-468.

   1934   Meikyoku Kaidai. Revised edition. Osaka:
          Mayakawa Gomei Kaisha, Inc.

   1956   Meikyoku Kaidai. Itami: Kamigata Kyodo
          Geijitsu Hozonkai.

Garfias, Robert
   1965   The Tōgaku Style of Japanese Court Music: An
          Analysis of Theory in Practice. Ph.D. diss.,
          University of California, Los Angeles.
             Forthcoming as: Music of a Thousand Autumns.
          Berkeley: University of California Press.

Harich-Schneider, Eta
   1973   A History of Japanese Music. London: Oxford
          University Press.

Hayashi, Kenzō
   n.d.   "Koto no chōgen no gensoku to hatten" ["Princi-
          ples and the Development of Koto Tuning"].
          Periodical unknown, pp. 83-131. Housed at the
          Archive of the Institute of Ethnomusicology,
          University of California, Los Angeles.

Keene, Donald
   1955   Anthology of Japanese Literature. New York:
          Grove Press.

Kishibe, Shigeo
    1957   Lecture notes, Seminar on Japanese Music,
            University of California, Los Angeles.

    1969   The Traditional Music of Japan. Revised edi-
            tion. Tokyo: Kokusai Bunka Shinkokai.

Kitahara, Michio
    1966   "Kayokyoku: An Example of Syncretism Involving
            Scale and Mode," Ethnomusicology, 10: 3,
            pp. 271-284.

Knott, C. G.
    1891   "Remarks on Japanese Musical Scales," Trans-
            actions of the Asiatic Society of Japan, 19,
            pp. 372-392.

Malm, William Paul
    1959   Japanese Music and Musical Instruments. Rut-
            land, Vermont: Charles E. Tuttle Company.

    1963   Nagauta: the Heart of Kabuki Music. Rutland,
            Vermont: Charles E. Tuttle Company.

    1972   "On the Meaning and Invention of the Term
            'Disphony,'" Ethnomusicology, 16: 2, pp. 247-
            249.

Nakauchi, Chojo and Tamura Nishio
    1924   Koto-uta Oyobi Jiuta Zenshū. Tokyo: Ogawa
            Kikumatsu.

Nippon Gakujutsu Shinkokai
    1955   The Noh Drama. Ten plays from the Japanese
            selected and translated by the special Noh
            committee, Japanese classics translation
            committee. Rutland, Vermont: Charles E.
            Tuttle Company.

Ongaku Jiten
    1955-57 [Encyclopedia of Music]. Tokyo: Heibonsha.
            12 volumes.

Piggott, Sir Francis
    1909   The Music and Musical Instruments of Japan.
            Second edition. London: B. T. Batsford.
            New York: Da Capo Press, 1971, Reprint.

Sadler, A. L., transl.
    1941   The Heike Monogatari. Tokyo: Kimiwada Shoten.

Saikaku Ihara
    1956   Five Women Who Loved Love. Translated by
            William Theodore DeBary. Rutland, Vermont:
            Charles E. Tuttle Company.

    1972a   Comrade Loves of the Samurai. Translated by
            E. Powys Mathers. Rutland, Vermont: Charles
            E. Tuttle Company.

    1972b   The Ten Foot Square Hut and Tales of the Heike.
            Translated by A. L. Sadler. Rutland,
            Vermont: Charles E. Tuttle Company.

Smith, Bradley
    1964   Japan: A History in Art. Introduction to the
            History of Japan by Marius B. Jansen. Intro-
            duction to the Art of Japan by Nagatake Asano.
            Garden City, New York: Doubleday and Co.

Staff (Editorial) of the Department of History of
            the Tozan School
    1932   History of the Tozan School. Tokyo: Rinzo
            Nakao.

Tafuki Seifu. Koshino Eisho, and Nakanoshima Shosen,
            eds.
    1933   Yamada Ryu Koto Uta Hachiyoshu. Fifth edition.
            Tokyo: Sokyoku Hachiyokai.

Tanabe Hisao and Yoshikawa Eishi
    1963   "Kifuho," Ongaku Jiten, 1. Tokyo: Heibonsha
            Publishing Company.

Tanabe Hisao
    1931   "Music in Japan." In Western Influences in
            Modern Japan. Chicago: University of Chicago
            Press, pp. 469-523.

Tanaka Giichi
    1963   Gendai Sokyoku Choshi Jiten. Osaka: Maekawa
            Suppansha.

Toyotaka Komiya, ed.
    1956   Japanese Music and Drama in the Meiji Era.
            Translated and adapted by Edward Seidensticker
            and Donald Keene. Tokyo: Obunsha.

Tsunoda Ryusaku, William Theodore DeBary, and Donald
            Keene, eds.
    1958   Sources of Japanese Tradition. New York:
            Columbia University Press. 2 volumes.

Uehara Rokushiro
    1927   Zokugaku Senritsu-ko。 Tokyo: Iwanami Bukusho。

Yoshikawa, Eiji, ed.
    1956   The Heike Story。 Translated by Fuki Uramatsu。
            New York: Alfred A。 Knopf.

Wakameda T。, transl。
    1922   Early Japanese Poets: Complete Translation of
            the Kokinshū。 Introduction by Kobayashi I.
            London: The Eastern Press, Ltd.

Waley, Arthur, transl。
    1955   The Tale of Genji. By Lady Murasaki。 New
            York: Doubleday Anchor Books.

Whitehouse, Wilfred and Yanagisawa Eizo, transl。
    1971   The Tale of the Lady Ochikubo. New York:
            Doubleday Anchor.

Scores

"Aki no Koto no Ha." Ikuta edition: Miyagi Michio, ed.
            for the Dai-Nihon Katei Ongakukai. Tokyo:
            Hōgakusha, 1971.

"Chidori no Kyoku." Ikuta edition: Miygai Michio, ed。
            for the Dai-Nihon Katai Ongakukai. Tokyo:
            Hōgakusha, 1964.

                        Yamada edition: Nakanoshima Kinichi,
            ed. Tokyo: Hōgakusha, 1963.

"Haru no Kyoku." Ikuta edition: Miyagi Michio, ed. for
            the Dai-Nihon Katei Ongakukai. Tokyo: Hōgaku-
            sha, 1971

"Saga no Aki." Ikuta edition, honte koto part: Yama-
            guchi Iwao, ed., for the Dai-Nihon Katei
            Ongakukai. Fukuoka: Hideo Sakamoto, 1961.

            Ikuta kaede koto part: In manuscript,
    on deposit at the Archive, Institute for Ethno-
    musicology, University of California at Los
    Angeles.

"Shin Takasago." Ikuta edition: Miyagi Michio, ed.,
            for the Dai-Nihon Katei Ongakukai. Tokyo:
            Hōgakusha, 1971。

Discography

Recordings of the five tegotomono studied herein
are difficult to find. Listed below are the few which
are readily available. In every case but one the compositions are incomplete; the entries below specify which
portions are performed. The "Chidori" performance is
the only one which includes the uta.

Japanese Koto Classics. Nonesuch H-72008. Ikuta ryū.
     "Chidori" Honte koto (Shinichi Yuize).
     Complete.

The Koto Music of Japan. Nonesuch HS-72005. Ikuta ryū.
     "Haru no Kyoku" Honte-kaede koto (Hagiwara
          Shogin and Mineuchi Ginsho) and shakuhachi
          (Kikusue). Mae-biki, Mae-jirashi (m. 137),
          Dan I, Dan II (Chirashi).

     "Shin Takasago" Honte koto with kaede part
          (some passages abridged) filled in by solo
          kotoist. Tegoto.

     On this record hear also "Godan Ginuta" (honte-
          kaede koto), "Rokudan" (honte koto) and
          "Yūgao" (Sankyoku).

Musical Treasures of Japan. Murray Hill Records S-4743.
     5 record set, one record of koto music. No artists
     mentioned.
          "Haru no Kyoku" Honte-kaede koto. Dan I
               from m. 162 where kaede enters to m. 307.

          "Aki no Koto no Ha" Honte-kaede koto. Tsunagi
               (m. 105) through Dan I.

          On this record hear also "Shōchikubai" (koto
               and shakuhachi).

The Soul of the Koto. Lyrichord LLST 7218. No artists
     mentioned.
          "Saga no Aki" Honte-kaede koto. Tegoto.

          On this record hear also "Rokudan" and "Kumoi
               Rokudan" (honte-kaede koto).

/ Index

ABOUT THE AUTHOR

Bonnie C. Wade, associate professor of music at the University of California, Berkeley, is an authority on the musics of Asia, particularly Japan and India. Among her other publications are *Introduction to Indian Classical Music* and *Khyal, Hindustani Classical Music*.